THE
ORVIS®
BOOK OF CABINS

THE
ORVIS®
BOOK OF CABINS

Amy Laughinghouse

THE LYONS PRESS

Guilford, Connecticut
An imprint of The Globe Pequot Press

Text © 2007 by Amy Laughinghouse
Photo credits: see page 174, which constitutes an extension of this page.
Pages i and 1: Artist's rendering of the Battenkill, one of Orvis Log Homes' cabins. Courtesy of Rocky Mountain Log Homes.
Page v: Photo © Brian Vanden Brink.
Page vi: Photo © Laurie E. Dickson Photography (detail, page 147).

Orvis is a registered trademark of The Orvis Company, Manchester, Vermont.
Visit Orvis at www.orvis.com.

The Lyons Press is an imprint of The Globe Pequot Press.

10 9 8 7 6 5 4 3 2 1

Printed in China

Designed by Nancy Freeborn
Layout by Peter Holm, Sterling Hill Productions
Project Editor: Marilyn Zelinsky-Syarto
Photo Editor: Anna Adesanya

Library of Congress Cataloging-in-Publication Data

Laughinghouse, Amy.
 The Orvis book of cabins / Amy Laughinghouse.
    p. cm.
 Includes bibliographical references and index.
 ISBN 978-1-59921-029-2 (alk. paper)
 1. Vacation homes—United States. 2. Log cabins—United States. I.
Orvis Company. II. Title.
 NA7575.L38 2007
 728.7'30973--dc22

A bear needs a
DEN
a bird needs a
NEST
and a man needs a
CABIN

<small>PAUL FERSEN</small>

Contents

Introduction

REALIZING THE DREAM

Over the years, I've lived and breathed cabins. A cabin is a retreat in many senses, a place of both relaxation and exploration. It is a release from the hectic demands of the twenty-first century, a haven in the woods where daily rhythms are influenced by sunrise and sunset, sunshine and snow—not only by conference calls and soccer practice. A cabin is a getaway where we allow ourselves to pay homage to the outdoors and enjoy simple, unscheduled pleasures, such as an early morning walk in the forest or an afternoon spent hip-deep in a mountain river, casting a fly rod into a current teaming with trout.

After writing about more than sixty log and timber frame homes across the country, I've realized my own vision of a little log getaway, having built one with my husband on an isolated peak east of Asheville, North Carolina. I don't just talk the talk when it comes to cabins. I walk the walk, hike the hikes, and like so many of the folks I've interviewed, I dream about the day when we can live full-time at our mountaintop retreat.

A wide pathway, flanked by trees clad in their New England autumn finery, extends a warm invitation and draws the eye towards this cabin sheathed in cedar shingles. With its steeply pitched gables, the little cabin seems to reach for the sky, while the gracious porch anchors it to this wooded peninsula.

THE QUALITIES OF A CABIN

Cabins can take many forms, from peaked-roof timber frames to rustic stick-framed enclosures. But there are several key elements common to true cabins: a rural setting; a simple, rustic design; natural building materials exposed for their innate beauty; and clever storage for the tools and equipment we need to participate in outdoor activities.

Location

Perhaps the most important factor is location. The desire to build a cabin is often fueled by invisible strings that draw us to a particular place. We may be inspired by the splendid isolation of a mountain peak, an unfurling vista of open plains, or the rippling melody of a swift-running stream. We stack the logs of our wilderness escape so we can feast our eyes upon the best views, or cock our ear to hear the whispered incantations of the river that lured us to that spot in the first place. Wherever we choose to build, we are mindful that a cabin should complement, never overwhelm, its surroundings.

From its perch at 2,900 feet, my cabin, located forty minutes east of Asheville, North Carolina, offers birds-eye views of the Blue Ridge Mountains. Looking out from this screened in porch, my husband and I often watch the birds soaring over the valley below us.

This log cabin on Maine's Rangeley Lake has been in the same family since the early twentieth century. The shady screened porch was recently added to provide a greater opportunity to enjoy the lake views. Wicker furnishings provide seating for extended family gatherings, and traditional braided rugs cushion the porch decking.

For more than a century, this golden valley has embraced a ranch where cattle graze in the company of elk, and deer and fox patrol the lush meadows. Painstakingly restored cabins gather alongside the edge of a stocked fishing pond, as if admiring their reflection against a backdrop of Colorado's snowcapped Sneffels Range.

Simplicity

The ideal cabin is unpretentious and uncomplicated. As Paul Fersen, a writer who is also a longtime Orvis employee, observes, "A cabin is quintessentially simplistic in that it offers the three things that you need in the wilderness: a roof to keep you dry, a fireplace to keep you warm, and a porch to keep you cool when it's hot."

Simplicity can mean modest square footage and fewer rooms. Bringing in the walls a few feet can actually help bring your family and friends closer as well, by fostering intimacy and promoting togetherness. At its most basic, a cabin may encompass little more than a sleeping loft and a great room that combines the kitchen, dining, and living areas.

In many cabins, amenities, too, are kept to a minimum. While few go so far as to eschew electricity and plumbing, satellite TV may prove an unnecessary distraction—as long as you've got plenty of dog-eared novels and board games on hand for rainy evenings. A cabin owner doesn't necessarily need a lot of bells and whistles—unless that "whistle" happens to be a duck call.

Building Materials

Building materials play a key role in making a cabin *feel* like a cabin. From the moment you step inside, a cabin should envelop you in the rich, earthy scent of wood, as if you'd never really closed the door on your surroundings. Features like log walls, wood paneling, stout timbers, heart-pine floors, and tongue-and-groove ceilings invite the outdoors over the threshold. Stone accents, such as a fireplace made of river rock worn smooth by the incessant caress of a stream, complement the wood while lending a sense of steadfastness and permanence that seems only right in a retreat that may be passed down for generations. To create the impression that a new cabin has already stood the test of time, many cabin owners incorporate salvaged materials, such as weathered old barn wood or a rusted tin roof.

This 1,200-square-foot cabin combines the living, dining, and kitchen areas in one cozy room. An antique Hoosier cabinet serves as a pantry, while a second hutch stores the dishes. A simple ladder leads to a sleeping loft overhead. Father and son worked sporadically for two years to finish the interior, although a railing for the overhead loft still remains on their "to do" list.

Situated at 7,400 feet among old-growth firs, this Montana cabin pays homage to its surroundings by incorporating twigs and round log fir accents harvested after a fire on the property. From the flagstone porch, which is topped by a gable faced in old barn wood, the owners can take in views of Lone Mountain or watch natural dramas unfold as grizzlies, black bear and herds of elk emerge from the forest around them.

The first thing many visitors to my North Carolina cabin comment upon is the scent of pine that perfumes the air, thanks to the rounded, kiln-dried log walls which enclose it. We selected pine flooring, stained a rich color to contrast with the honey-colored logs, to withstand mud and gravel dust tracked in from our hikes. Leather sofas, chosen for their durability and comfort, are centered around a cultured stone fireplace that boasts a sturdy oak mantel.

Sporting Collectibles

Antique hunting, fishing, and boating gear, as well as old sporting advertisements, are increasingly used in interiors as homeowners decide they want to live with objects that evoke their passions. Cabins in particular beg for this kind of display.

For many collectors, these items hold tremendous sentimental value, as they represent a tangible link to the great sporting traditions of the past. "They've got a connection to the old fishing creels of their grandfather's day," says Bob Murphy, an Orvis staffer who has done extensive research on sporting gear. "They've seen the bamboo fly rods in the closet, and they know the old pump shotgun that was in the garage with the cork decoys. There's an emotional connection," he explains.

Front and back views of a rare early twentieth-century British creel.

But beyond their nostalgic appeal, some antique sporting items have considerable monetary value, as well. Popular categories include:

:: Duck decoys
:: Fishing gear: fishing creels, bamboo fly rods, fly reels, fishing lures
:: Wildlife and sporting art: calendar art, advertising lithographs
:: Packaging: powder tins, shotgun shell boxes
:: Accessories: fishing badges, particularly from the South

In addition to the sporting collectibles available through Orvis, other potential sources include the Internet, flea markets, antiques shops, and auctions. When you're on the hunt, keep in mind that, as with most antiques, an item's value is typically determined by its condition, its rareness, and popular demand. For instance, an antique fishing lure with its original paint is generally worth more than one that has been repainted. With bamboo rods, beware of broken tips, bent rods, and poorer-quality rods that have been refitted with an expensive handle to mislead a buyer.

You can educate yourself by attending sports shows where these items are traded and sold and by studying books devoted to the subject. With greater knowledge comes a greater appreciation of their craftsmanship and their contribution to our collective sporting heritage.

Reproduction glass minnow trap, fly collection, contemporary "Big Sky" brown trout fish carvings, and reproduction fly reels. All are available through Orvis.

Accessories and Collectibles

But it's not just the walls, the floor, and the roof that define your cabin. It's what you put inside it, as well. If you build a hunting and fishing camp, then furnish it with pieces that can withstand a little wear and tear. Forget the flowery chintz sofa and Chinoiserie cocktail table, and opt instead for a comfortable leather armchair and a sturdy wooden coffee table where you can prop up your feet without taking off your boots.

When it comes to accessorizing, surround yourself with objects that evoke your sporting interests and convey a sense of history. Duck and fish decoys, ranging from early twentieth-century collectibles to limited edition reproductions, are works of art unto themselves. Even new gear can be displayed and then retrieved for use in the appropriate season. Showcase fishing lures in a shadow box, or hang your carved wooden canoe and paddles on the wall. Allow their utilitarian beauty and sleek efficiency to resound within your cabin, inspiring you to pursue the activities you love.

Rifles, glinting spurs, and a well-worn saddlebag are suspended from the reclaimed timbers which frame the study of this cabin.

A porch outfitted with a fireplace and picnic table embodies the ideal of indoor-outdoor cabin living—sheltered, but not isolated, from the elements.

AN ORVIS BOOK OF CABINS

Orvis is a company with a passion for outdoor pursuits. For more than 150 years, it has honored the Thoreau-like existence of cabin life. Charles F. Orvis founded the company in 1856 as a fly-fishing business, and the Perkins family, which purchased Orvis in 1965, has retained a focus on distinctive country living and all that entails, with an emphasis on the history and heritage of fly-fishing and hunting.

The company now also embraces the structures that embody the Orvis lifestyle. It selects and offers furnishings for the home. It collects and reproduces precious sporting artifacts for enjoyment in a home setting. And it has launched The Orvis Log Homes, a line of cabin designs built in conjunction with Rocky Mountain Log Homes, which include well-thought-out elements such as gun-and-rod storage, an area for

bathing and boarding your dog, and a work bench for fly tying. These are just the sort of practical ideas spotlighted in this book's features and in selected cabins, such as Jim and Karen Grace's home in Red Lodge, Montana. An all-seasons porch provides storage for Jim's fly-fishing gear, and the bathroom shower was deliberately oversized so the couple could bathe their two Newfoundland dogs, Retro and Daisy.

Understanding how Orvis values the desire to align ourselves with nature and experience the outdoors has led me to present the Grace's cabin, along with eighteen others that exemplify ideal cabin living. Like Orvis, these cabin owners respect the traditions of the past while living in the moment, adding their own chapters to a sporting history that will continue to unfold as long as there are trout in a stream.

At just over 1,500 square feet, the Battenkill is the smallest of the Orvis Log Homes' floor plans, yet it encompasses all the essentials. The Sportsman's Room features ample space for gear storage, as well as a kennel with a door leading directly to a dog run, and a multi-purpose great room combines the functions of cooking, dining, and relaxing around the fireplace, drawing families and friends together. A classic cabin bunk room creates a feeling of fellowship that hearkens back to the carefree days of summer camp, while a master suite above features a loft that connects it to the great room below. **Courtesy Rocky Mountain Log Homes**

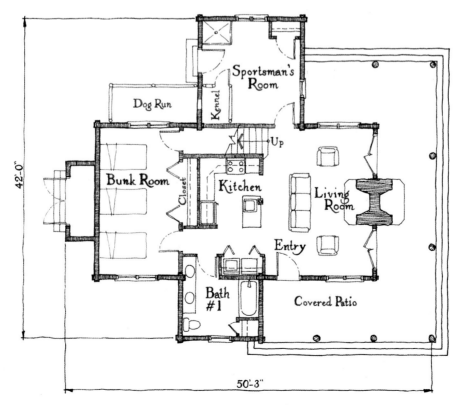

THE
ORVIS®
BOOK OF CABINS

Honoring the American Frontier

A memory lives on in the walls of this historic cabin

:: *"Cold was the night and bitter the wind and brutal the trail behind. Hunched in the saddle, I growled at the dark and peered through the blinding rain."*

So begins "Here Ends the Trail," a short story by one of America's most prolific and popular writers, the late Louis L'Amour. His protagonists were often lonely men with a hard past searching for shelter, and more than that . . . a home. L'Amour would eventually find his own peace in an historic log cabin nestled in the La Plata Mountains outside Durango, Colorado. There, he immersed himself in the solace of nature with his wife, Kathy, and their two children, Beau and Angelique.

"Louis had an incredible passion for reading," says Kathy, who added built-in shelves as part of their log home renovation. Today, the shelves are filled with a collection of L'Amour's own leather bound novels. A silver framed photo features Kathy and Louis enjoying a quiet moment on their front porch.

ENCOUNTERING THE ELEMENTS

"Louis loved doing physical things, like clearing out the oak brush and chopping it up," says Kathy, whose husband was 75 years old when they bought the ranch in 1983. "He liked examining the terrain, hiking on it, and seeing what lived there. We have all kinds of wild animals—deer, elk, bear, coyotes, mountain lions, skunks," she says. "Louis just enjoyed being out in the elements. The weather and terrain were big characters in his novels. They played an important role in the whole settling of the West."

The ranch was ostensibly a getaway from their main residence in Los Angeles, yet L'Amour still rose at 5:30 every morning, pecking away at his IBM Selectric for six hours or more a day. "He loved sitting at the old pine table that he used for a desk, looking out at the meadow, the pond, the weeping willow, and the peony patch I planted," Kathy remembers. In fact, L'Amour, the author of more than 200 short stories and nearly 100 novels, wrote several novels here before his death in 1988, including *The Haunted Mesa* and *Passin' Through*, which is set on the ranch itself.

"Louis loved to sit there on the porch and have his coffee and look out at the mountains," recalls Susan Brown, an old family friend and interior designer whom Kathy enlisted to help her furnish the cabin.

THE LONG ROAD HOME

Though he did finally put down roots, L'Amour knew what it was like to be a wandering soul, for, like his heroes, he had taken the long road home. Born in Jamestown, North Dakota, in 1908, he left school in the tenth grade. He struck out on his own to make a living just as the devastating stranglehold of the Great Depression began to grip the Midwest.

"He had a tough life," recalls Kathy, who married L'Amour in 1956. "He had gone to sea, worked in mines, worked on ranches, worked in the lumber country. He never had a home, because times were tough and his family was always on the move. He was alone for a lot of his life."

During those hard, lean years, L'Amour's job description ranged from longshoreman to professional boxer to elephant handler. But his wide-ranging travels brought him in contact with larger-than-life characters—legendary lawmen and outlaws, real-life cowboys and Native Americans. Their tales, coupled with his grandfather's first-hand recollections of life on the Western frontier, fueled L'Amour's imagination.

After World War II, where he served as an officer in the European theater, L'Amour eventually began penning Westerns which, given his background, he seemed destined to write. By the time *Hondo*—the story of a dispatch rider, later immortalized on film by John Wayne—was published in 1953, he was already on the road to success.

RETURN TO DURANGO

He continued to work ceaselessly, writing an average of three books a year and crisscrossing the country on research trips with his wife and children in tow. "Louis wanted to look and feel, taste, and understand the terrain, the culture, the people, and their history," Kathy explains.

But one place the family returned to again and again was Durango, Colorado. "We started spending a big chunk of our summers here with the children in

"Durango has managed to preserve the great things of the 19th century," says Kathy, who has renovated and redecorated five homes on her own property as she has expanded the ranch.

the 1960s," Kathy recalls. "It's just a perfect little town with wonderful old architecture. It sits between four Indian reservations, right in the middle of horse country, cow country, sheep country, timber country, mining country. It has gorgeous weather and beautiful terrain—everything we were interested in. We just loved the people and the town and the uniqueness of the setting."

The only thing it didn't seem to have was the right ranch at the right price. For nearly twenty years, the L'Amours searched for their home away from home.

"We just kept looking and looking, and one day, we drove down into this ranch, and it was covered in snow," Kathy says, conjuring images of that frigid winter afternoon in 1983. "It had a beautiful high ridge, a little creek running through it, and lovely meadows. We fell in love with it, made an offer in the spring—and bought it!"

REVEALING HIDDEN TREASURES

The ranch originally consisted of 1,000 acres stretching along an old stage-coach road. There was a barn, a granary, and the log home itself, all built by a cattle rancher in 1881. It had been the site of Indian battles and apparently gunfights, as well. The L'Amours found the massive hand-hewn pine logs riddled with bullets.

Inside, the logs had been covered with paneling, which the L'Amours removed, revealing discolored logs, crumbling chinking, and a few other surprises. "People used to stuff all kinds of things in there to fill that deep hole (between the logs)—fabric, old newspapers, letters—anything that was at hand," Kathy explains.

In the living room, a pair of knuckle arm sofas, dressed in a plaid fabric, flank a rustic coffee table that is topped by a Navajo rug and antique Maidu and Yosemite Miwok baskets. *The Creation*, a painting by Native American artist Clifford Brycelea, takes pride of place on the mantel.

Louis L'Amour set his novel, *Passin' Through*, on the ranch that he and his wife Kathy bought in 1983. Nestled in a verdant valley, the ranch flanks an old stage coach road that was probably the same path used by Father Escalante during his historic expedition from Santa Fe to Utah in 1776.

The L'Amours assembled a team, including architect Edward Carson Beall, project architect Frank Balogh, and builder Jim Messersmith, to oversee the necessary renovations. In addition to removing the interior paneling, sand-blasting the logs, and rechinking the home inside and out, the L'Amours installed new windows, converted one of four upstairs bedrooms into two bathrooms, enlarged the master bath to house a tub, and added a garage that connects to the home via a covered breezeway.

They also erected a dramatic fireplace of local stone, accented by a wide pine mantel made from a

Jim Rey's painting of a horse-drawn wagon presents the perfect complement to an antique cricket table topped by an old tooled-leather letter box and a lamp fashioned from a silver coffee pot that was once used on the transcontinental railroad.

tree they found on their own property, and raised the height of the opening between the living room and the dining room. "My son is 6 feet 4 inches—and he's nearly 7 feet tall when he's got on his hats and boots," Kathy explains. "Beau stood there while we measured and cut the entrance," she recalls with a laugh.

NOOKS FOR BOOKS

And, of course, the L'Amours needed to add bookshelves—lots of them—to house a portion of Louis' extensive library. "He had to have books," notes Kathy's friend Susan Brown, an accomplished actress as well as an interior designer whom the L'Amours enlisted to help decorate the home. But beyond that simple desire, says Brown, founder of Addison Interiors, he left the décor up to her and Kathy. "He was just a very dear person, wonderfully tolerant of whatever we brought in," recalls Brown, who worked with Kathy to select pine antiques and comfortable, practical furnishings accented by Navajo weavings and Native American baskets, as well as artwork by Clifford Brycelea, Jim Rey, and sculptors Veryl Goodnight and Star York.

Although L'Amour passed away in 1988, Kathy still returns to Durango often with her children and her grandchildren—hiking, fishing, and horseback riding. But Louis L'Amour, in a sense, never left. His memory lives on in the photos on his old desk, the volumes of his work that fill the bookshelves, and the rocking chair where he once sat and sipped his coffee, savoring the same satisfaction he liked to award his heroes.

"So we went in and the coffee was hot and black," L'Amour concludes in *Here Ends the Trail*, "and there by the table there was warm and pleasant talk of cattle and grass and what a man could do in a green growing valley, with time on his hands."

Louis L'Amour's publisher presented him with this king-sized quilt, embroidered with the names of his books, in 1982. Although L'Amour passed away in 1988, all of his titles are still in print.

Kathy and Louis L'Amour entertained a wide circle of friends at their dinner parties, from local artists and Hollywood entertainers to the former Librarian of Congress. "I still love to cook and get interesting people together," Kathy says.

A Celestial Ski Retreat

Finding a base camp for an outdoor lifestyle

:: Perched on a high ridge between four majestic peaks in Big Sky, Montana, Ben and Paula Blend's log home is a welcome oasis of warmth, a refuge of cozy comfort tucked among snow-laden pines. Gray clouds ride in over the west, bringing blizzards that cloak the country in a blanket of white. But the Blends are happy to weather the storms amid the massive cedar logs in a home that lies, quite literally, at the end of the rainbow.

"Usually, after it rains, we have double rainbows behind the house," explains Paula. "And once or twice, over Sphinx Mountain, we've seen a big, wide rainbow pointing straight down."

To take advantage of their picture-postcard views of Montana's mountain peaks, the Blends used aeronautical cable in place of wooden balusters on their porch. The decking is made of recycled plastic. "There is no maintenance to it at all," Paula says.

The cabin features colorful artwork mixed with Western memorabilia, including a saddle that once belonged to Paula's father. Twenty-four-inch square slate tile flooring, warmed by radiant heating, stands up well to snowy boots. In the living room, a large plate glass window frames a view of Lone Mountain, a popular ski slope.

WAITING FOR A SIGN

Unfortunately, when Paula and Ben were ready to trade in their Dallas home for a full-time wilderness retreat, there were no celestial symbols pointing the way. For four years, they methodically searched the Midwest and the Northwest, seeking a town that tickled their fancy. Then, late one night, the Blends stopped for dinner in Montana, and a waitress suggested they check out property in Big Sky. From there, they followed the signs—literally—and stopped in at the realty office with the biggest billboards.

Their realtor showed them a 10-acre parcel, 8,220 feet above sea level, where builder Doug Bing had planned to erect a spec home. The Blends met with Bing, and bingo! The deal was sealed.

SHOWCASING PANORAMIC VIEWS

Their mountain aerie would prove the perfect base camp for an outdoor lifestyle, which they have adapted to fit the climate. The Blends used to water ski in Texas; they have now learned to snow ski in Montana. "We're so close to the slopes, it's practically a sin not to ski," Paula says. They've taken up fly-fishing, too, and they've adopted a border collie-Australian shepherd mix, Jax, to accompany them on their frequent hikes in the Spanish Peaks, Gallatin Canyon, and Yellowstone.

Even their home takes full advantage of its surroundings, incorporating 30-inch western red cedar logs, huge picture windows, and nearly 800 feet of decking to showcase the panoramic views. Fieldstone accents around the foundation of the home visually anchor it to the site, and slab cedar siding with a chink joint encases the rustic exterior. Inside, timber-framed cathedral ceilings soar above the great room. Twenty-four-inch slate tile flooring and recycled barn wood, reincarnated as kitchen cabinets and great room cupboards, create a rough-and-ready framework.

A constant theme throughout the home is Paula's artwork. Her paintings range from an abstract vision of a lake ringed by flowers that graces the stairwell to a realistic rendition of an iceberg, based on a photo taken in Antarctica, which hangs over the fireplace. Moving to Big Sky has actually changed the focus of her paintings, Paula says. "I'm doing more animals and landscapes now than I used to," she explains. "It's a more traditional style of painting, and the landscapes are more towards the classical end."

Wide overhangs and massive logs, 30 inches in diameter, hearken back to classic national park architecture. The flared bases of the western red cedar logs add an organic element to the columns supporting the front porch. Builder Doug Bing likes working with this species not only because of the size and shape of the logs, but because the wood is naturally insect resistant.

Inspiration is just outside the window, whether Paula and Ben are watching the sun set behind the mountains or observing a heard of elk meandering across the ridge. "We have all kind of animals, the same ones you would see at Yellowstone," says Paula, who has spotted deer, grizzly and black bear, a female moose with her spring calf, and a marmot family that's taken up residence in their brush pile. "We have everything but Old Faithful in our front yard."

Paula's art studio fills the space above the garage. Dormers grant the room much-needed headspace, while a slanted, triangular bookshelf plays off of the room's architectural angles.

Two oversized, Crayola-colored armchairs cozy up to a fieldstone fireplace. Cabinets made of salvaged barn wood flank the fireplace, which is a pass-through design shared by the master bedroom.

Choosing a Site

Once you've resolved to find a cabin getaway of your own, one of the most important decisions you'll make is where to build it. A home, after all, comprises more than the four walls that enclose it. It is defined by the natural beauty that lies beyond those walls, as well.

If time permits, get to know your land during all four seasons. Chart the path of the sun to determine how you might benefit from its warmth in winter without baking in the summer heat.

:: Views. Note how the views change throughout the year. When the branches are stark and naked against the sky, you may discover a distant vista you never knew was there. Consider how you might position your cabin windows to frame not only the obvious views, such as a snow-capped summit, but more subtle discoveries, too, such as the flaming red leaves of a dogwood in autumn.

:: Water. Walk the property to see if there are streams that need to be accommodated and how this might work to your advantage. One couple actually built their home to straddle a creek, and they installed plenty of windows to welcome indoors the sights and sounds of the surrounding woods. Be sure, however, that you don't build on a floodplain.

:: Conserve. Take stock of favorite trees or rare plants that you want to preserve and mark them for your general contractor. Let your construction crew know if you wish to save large boulders that could be used for landscaping.

:: Approach. Once you've decided where to build, consider the best way to position the approach for your driveway. The most favorable path to your site may not be the most direct. A slight detour past a meadow or around a patch of mountain laurel could set the mood before you even reach the front door.

Views can be "framed" both inside and out, through the placement of furnishings and windows. A scenic spot becomes a destination for contemplation and relaxation with a bench or a pair of comfortable chairs.

Polishing a 1920s Lakeside Gem

A neglected cabin gets a makeover

:: Ken and Sue Bergman's renovated log cabin sits atop a hill offering spectacular sunset vistas and is sited 150 feet away from a sapphire-blue lake in Minnesota. A scenic point 500 feet from the front door overlooks a pair of distant islands, while a tranquil bay a short walk away offers first-rate fishing among the wild rice and lily pads. It's the perfect vacation home for this active couple—yet the cabin is nothing like what they'd first envisioned.

"We were looking for something low-maintenance and ready to move into—something simple," Ken recalls. "And I wanted neighbors close by," Sue adds.

Needless to say, things didn't go exactly as planned.

A bi-level deck leads to a wide pea gravel path, sloping down to a 900-acre glacial lake. The new daylight basement is topped by an addition encompassing a master suite and entry hall.

As part of their renovation, Ken and Sue added a new front entry, leading into a spacious hall just off the new kitchen.

When Ken and Sue bought this lakeside property, they thought the old stone fireplace might be the only portion of the original cabin worth saving. But their change of heart led to an eleven-year renovation process. Today, a new addition—including the screened porch next to the fireplace—blends beautifully with the restored cabin.

A RARE PROPERTY

In the summer of 1993, Ken's uncle mentioned a 24-acre plot for sale on a 900-acre lake two hours from their home in the Minneapolis–St. Paul area. The lot featured a 1920s log cabin that had been deserted for 12 years. Nearly 20 percent of the logs had dry rot, and the porch was on the verge of collapse. There was not a neighbor's house in sight—just a primitive guest cottage, an outhouse, and a garage that once doubled as a homespun maple syrup factory, all tucked among a jungle of overgrown bushes and weeds. The site was the polar opposite of what the Bergmans thought they wanted in a getaway, and yet, Sue says, "It felt like it was meant to be."

"It was so peaceful," she notes, explaining her abrupt about-face. "You couldn't see anything or hear anything, and to find a lot of property on a lake is such a rarity."

"We made an offer that day, without ever going inside the cabin," Ken confesses. "If the price was right, we didn't care if the cabin was there or not."

The couple initially intended to tear down the cabin and preserve only the original fireplace—a massive structure boasting multihued, weather-worn stones and an old metal hook that once held a cook pot over the flames. "But with time," Ken says, "instead of looking at the 20 percent that was really bad, we started looking at the 80 percent that was still good—so we decided to try to salvage the whole structure."

PRESERVING A TIME CAPSULE

The previous owner had simply locked the door and walked away in the early 1980s, leaving a fully furnished time capsule behind. The beds were made. The pantry was stocked, and the cabinets were filled with long-expired medications.

As Ken hacked away at the underbrush, Sue sorted through furniture and accessories, salvaging whatever she could. "It was like discovering little gems," says Sue, who gave several items to their two grown sons as

well as Ken's aunt and uncle. She kept a few odds and ends, such as antique dishes, to use in the cabin. "We wanted to have that reminder of what was there before—to preserve a bit of the history," she explains.

For the first four years, as they struggled to prepare the cabin for habitation, Ken and Sue stayed in the guest cottage during their weekend visits. "It was darling," Sue insists, "but we shared it with mice and bats." The cottage had electricity but no plumbing. Ken installed a chemical toilet in a closet, but if they wanted a bath, they waded into the lake. "I felt like a pioneer woman!" Sue recalls with a laugh.

CRAFTING A CIVILIZED RETREAT

In 1995, with the property taking shape and the cabin's interior cleaned and tidied, Ken and Sue consulted with architect Katherine Hillbrand. Hillbrand was recommended by a log home builder who remembered

playing in the old cabin as a boy. The resulting blueprints preserved as much of the antique structure as possible, while tripling the square footage with a new addition and creating an open, light-filled floor plan. The designs also featured a loft, which serves as extra sleeping quarters and the grandchildren's playroom, and included not just one bathroom, but two.

It was a modest, comfortable plan—exactly what Ken and Sue required for their North Woods retreat. "But we wanted at least some of the comforts of home—like showers and flushing toilets," Ken adds.

A local craftsman created these custom black ash cabinets with old-fashioned bead-board paneling that even hides the refrigerator. To the left of the stove, a window from the original cabin now looks into a bright new foyer. "It gives me much more a feeling of space," Sue says of her portal. Leaf-print Formica counters complement the cabin's rich wood tones.

The cabin's 1922 fireplace, featuring the original mantel inscribed with a line from James Russell Lowell's poem "The Courtin,'" serves as the focal point of the living room. "We felt we had to preserve that part of history," Ken says. A framed copy of the poem—a housewarming gift from a cousin—takes pride of place between the mantel and a pine hutch from Sue's mother.

here warn't no stoves (tell comfort died) To bake ye to a puddin'

To prepare for the building process, Ken signed up for a 10-day log building course in Isabella, Minnesota. "It allowed me to do some work as we went along and to talk intelligently with people involved with the project, but mostly that school taught me that I better get help with the project," Ken admits with a laugh.

He eventually hired general contactor Dan Heikklia and a former classmate, Rudy Salie, who has been building log homes since the 1970s. Ken still contributed considerable sweat equity, such as solvent-washing the original interior. As he balanced himself on planks between rafters to reach the cathedral ceiling, he revealed a beautiful golden stain that had been dulled by years of grime. He found a company to custom match the antique stain for the new addition and began the process of sanding the new logs inside and out to achieve a rustic look. After removing the old chinking—a crumbling mixture of horsehair, moss, and tar—and restaining the exterior, Ken replaced the chinking with a water-based, synthetic polymer sealant that he shaped using a cake-decorating spatula.

Sue furnished the home with treasured country pieces passed down from her mother, mixed with rustic accents such as an Amish rocker, a pair of bent willow chairs, and a bear cub table base carved from redwood. "My theory is that you shouldn't buy everything together and have it all match," explains Sue, who prefers to combine well-loved pieces that have a history.

"We're proud of the cabin because we utilized what was there, versus just smashing it down and starting from scratch," she says of their cabin. "It's been a fabulous journey." Sometimes, it seems, there's a lot to be said for unexpected detours.

Rotted logs from the original home were removed to make way for gracious French doors that lead from the living room to the new screened porch. "In the summer, we have every meal on the porch," says Sue, who ordered custom striped awnings to shelter them during heavy rains.

Thanks to a custom stain, the new master bedroom boasts the same golden glow as the logs from the original cabin. Sue chose a dainty iron bed frame, without a box spring, to lend old-fashioned charm while taking up minimal space. A wooden filing cabinet does double-duty as a bedside table, as the room also serves as a small office.

A wide, gracious deck replaced the crumbling old screened porch, which once cast the house in shadow. Large new windows also supplanted the small original windows throughout the home, filling the cabin with light.

Detailing Doorways

A cabin doorway can be more than a passage. It can say a great deal about you and the image you wish to convey to the world. Even if your home is built from a kit or from a widely published house plan, your entryway is your opportunity to personalize it and make a vital first impression about what your home means to you.

:: Be playful. At a cabin, which is often a second home set in the wilderness, a door can be much more creative than it might be at a formal home in the city or the suburbs.

:: Proclaim your interests. If you have an affinity for wildlife, that idea can be easily expressed with a door featuring an animal carving, for example.

:: Send a message. You can spell out your message in words. ("Abandon all hope, ye who enter here" engraved upon the lintel ought to dissuade mischievous trick-or-treaters). Or, add sidelights and a transom to foster a sense of welcome while simultaneously mustering a bit of intrigue.

:: Be inviting. An unusual-shaped doorway opening or one encased by character logs draws the eye and beckons your visitors to enter and explore.

:: Create a frame. An open doorway can be used to visually frame an object, such as a painting or a mounted trophy fish, in the room beyond.

Facing page: Massive wood-plank doors lead beneath an arched lintel to a staging area for chaps, cowboy hats, and other essential ranching gear. Although the doors are made of simple planks, the iron hardware, including diamond-shaped studs and three sets of hinges, give the entrance weight and substance.

Top left: An original door to a calving barn dates back to a homestead settled more than a century ago in southwestern Colorado. The iron hardware, which bears Centennial Ranch's circle-star emblem, is new, but its hand-forged origins lend it a patina that hearkens back to the West's pioneering days.

Bottom left: This passage to the foyer of a log home in Casco Bay, Maine, was enhanced by an on-site alteration made by the builder. Using a chain saw, he carved an arch into an interior log wall, mirroring an archway on the opposite wall. The balusters on the stairway are made of white cedar twigs.

Bottom right: A painted relief of a deer in this Pennsylvania mountain home attests to the owners' interest in the local fauna. Although this is an interior doorway, the cultured stone wall creates the illusion that the deer is peeking inside from the woods beyond.

Creating a Cabin Guest House

A rustic retreat proves too irresistible to reserve for visitors

:: On the outskirts of Jackson, Wyoming, a snug cabin clings to the steep slope of West Gros Ventre Butte. The creaking of a rocking chair on the sandstone patio accompanies the rustling of wildflowers on warm spring days, while inside, the percussive symphony of ricocheting billiard balls is interrupted by an occasional outburst of triumphant laughter.

With its lightly peeled antique logs, rough-sawn floors, and deliberate disconnection from many modern "amenities," this guest cabin is decidedly more rustic than the main residence 40 yards away. But for the Texas-based family that has made this breezy bluff their home away from home, this tiny outbuilding—composed of two 70-year-old log cabins joined by a central stick-framed core—is the ultimate escape from the twenty-first century.

The stone patio has become a favorite respite for Neal, who often adjourns here with a book in fine weather.

BLENDING INTO THE LANDSCAPE

Neal and Nancy McManne, the parents of three teenage children, were originally attracted to Jackson Hole by its variety of outdoor activities and its prolific wildlife, which includes a steady parade of eagles, elk, moose, bear, and bison. The whole family enjoys skiing, hiking, canoeing, rafting, and fly-fishing, and their son has also developed an interest in glacier climbing. "We wanted a place where we could build family memories as our kids grew up, and where they could eventually bring their own children," Nancy says.

In 2001, the couple pounced on a 12-acre parcel atop a butte with 360-degree views of the mountains and the twinkling lights of Jackson below. After renovating an existing home on the site, adding log siding and stone accents to make it blend in seamlessly with the rugged environment, they turned their attention to building a new guesthouse that would double as a recreation room and casual clubhouse.

The couple opted to use antique logs for the structure because they not only complemented the log siding on the main house, but also because they

The sitting room features the original cathedral ceiling, which creates a feeling of spaciousness and height. An old butter churn by the window has been wired to function as a lamp.

simply "fit the feel" of Jackson, Nancy says. Fortunately, their general contractors were able to locate two small 1930s-era log cabins, each measuring approximately 14 by 18 square feet, that could be adapted for use in building the new home.

The cabins—which were lifted intact onto the foundation using a giant crane—were just the right size to house a bedroom and a sitting room. A central stick-

"When the builders were working on the old cabins to integrate them into the new structure, they had to remove some portions of logs, which we asked them to re-use to the extent that they could," Neal says. Those scraps were used to make benches and coat racks and as accents at the corners of the bar and entry hall.

framed core connects the cabins and encompasses a large game room with a kitchenette/bar, a small entryway, and a full bath, per the blueprints of architect Eliot Goss.

CRAFTING AN ANTIQUE RUSTIC INTERIOR

For an authentic 1930s look, the exterior of the stick-framed core was clad in vertical cedar boards and pine battens. "That's what would have been used on cabin construction in that era, if you had a portion of the cabin that wasn't log," Neal explains.

The interior of the stick-framed portion is entirely made of rough-sawn fir, which was used for the walls, ceiling, floor, counters, and trim. "Everything was intended to be rustic," Goss maintains. "Not 'Jackson Hole' rustic, which tends to be pretty elegant and expensive, but true rustic."

Most of the fir was left untreated, allowing it to develop its own natural patina over time. Only the random-width wide-planked flooring—which runs throughout the entire house—received a light stain. Yet it, too, is deliberately low-maintenance. "We wanted people to be able to walk in there wearing their ski boots," explains Nancy, who simply sweeps them clean.

The couple took the same "less is more" approach with the cabins, preserving as much of their original look as possible, from the interior wood chinking to the "scars" left by previous owners. "There are places in the logs that are notched, where someone decided to hang a picture or a mirror," Nancy admits, "but we decided that's part of the charm."

In fact, Neal and Nancy view the logs as art unto themselves—and they've "framed" them accordingly. The opening from the rec room into the sitting room, for instance, showcases what was once the exterior log wall of the old cabin, revealed by an oversized cutout in the stick-framed wall. Cathy Chapman of Chapman Design Inc., the Houston-based interior designer who helped Neal and Nancy furnish the home, also placed empty "tramp art" frames (art that wandering souls made for money during the Great Depression) on the log walls. "We just let the logs show through," Chapman explains. "It's kind of primitive and fun."

A REFUGE OF WARMTH

To enhance the look of the logs and rough-sawn fir, Chapman devised an autumnal palette of red, gold, and sage green, which appears in striped, floral, plaid, and leaf-printed fabrics throughout the home. "[The décor] needs to be very warm-toned—nothing crisp," she warns.

Weathering the Challenges

Building atop a windy mountain in the dead of winter provided a daunting set of challenges for the construction team. Snow piled up in the foundation, and the protective tarps that sheltered the site were ripped to shreds by the wind.

But the weather—which occasionally left the crew snowed in at the steep, muddy site—wasn't the only foe. Two antique cabins had to be hauled up the mountain on trailers, and the only crane big enough to lift them onto the foundation had to be imported from Idaho.

Yet despite these hurdles, the crew finished the cabin on time in July 2004—and the hard-won battles made the fruits of their labor seem that much sweeter. The homeowners believe the result is a work of art.

While the lone bedroom is cozily equipped with antiques and reproduction pieces, the game room, by contrast, is sparingly furnished, with little more than a pool table, poker table, and a few small log chairs. "You have to have a lot of space around the pool table," Chapman says. "It's all about function."

The adjacent sitting room, however, is all about warmth—both literal and figurative. A wood-burning stove glows in the corner and is meant to supplement the electric baseboard heat. Visual warmth is provided by a custom-made rolled-arm leather and chenille sofa accompanied by two comfortable armchairs. Unusual accents, such as a lamp constructed from a butter churn and a rug with a bison design Neal found in Jackson, complete a vignette too inviting to reserve only for guests.

"A few times I haven't known where Neal is, and I find him just hanging out down there," Nancy reveals with a laugh. "As much as Jackson Hole is a getaway for us, if we really want to get away, we go to the cabin."

In the bedroom, a red armoire takes the place of a built-in closet, which would never be found in an historic cabin. Above the bed, a "tramp art" mirror and empty wooden frame draw attention to the rustic log walls.

Creating Antique Patina

There is something undeniably attractive about the notion that a cabin has withstood the ravages of time and yet has still held fast to its foundation. But even if your home was built yesterday, there are timeless techniques that can lend it the patina of yesteryear.

:: **Recycled wood.** One of the most common ways to amplify a home's age is to incorporate recycled wood. Beams salvaged from barns, bridges, or old warehouses can be reconfigured as trusses or sawed into planks for siding, paneling, hardwood floors, and cabinetry.

:: **Antique house parts.** Likewise, rescuing and reusing antique windows and doors will add years of well-worn adornment to your cabin's appearance.

:: **Distressing.** You can also give new construction a "make-older" makeover with a little sweat equity. Take cabinet doors and lightly hammer in nail holes to give them a time-worn look, and chip new bricks to make them appear as if they have long endured the wind and the rain. For painted cabinets with an antiqued finish, cover furniture first with watered-down latex paint and then sand lightly once the paint has dried.

:: **Using chemicals.** Other tricks of the trade speed up the natural processes of aging and erosion by employing chemicals. Muriatic acid and pressure-washing rust a metal roof in record time, while soda-blasting and a watered-down solution of ferrous sulfate can produce weathered plank siding that passes for old barn wood. If you can't find antique hardware, soak new hinges and nails in an open vat of vinegar to promote rust. (Note: Never soak metal in a closed container of acidic fluid because gases may cause the container to burst. Always wear protective gear, such as goggles and gloves, when handling chemicals.)

By evoking a sense of history, whether real or imagined, you can set the stage for an unforgettable escape where you'll create your own memories—today, tomorrow, and in the years to come.

Facing page, top left: The wood paneling in this Montana home has had more lives than a cat. It was originally used to build an airplane hangar, then reclaimed for a lumber mill before finally coming to rest here in Bigfork. In keeping with this search and rescue theme, the owner also ferreted out a decorative antique transom to adorn this doorway

Facing page, top right: An 1830s three-bay barn was disassembled and transported to Stowe, Vermont, where it was reassembled to house this family's dining area.

Facing page, bottom: All the wood in this Douglas fir timber frame was recycled from an early 19th century sawmill in Washington state. Here in the study, the wood was left rough and weathered, just as it was found when it was salvaged.

Below: An old terra cotta mop sink, a salvaged wood vanity, and rusted roof panels used in place of paneling create a pioneer-style bathroom in Otto, North Carolina.

A Simple Boat House

An "unfinished" cabin encourages a couple to live an
uncomplicated life, both on and off the water

:: Given Tom and Ann Chapman's love of the water, building a cabin
that doubles as a boat house seemed as natural to them as selecting a site
along Maine's pebbly shore. Their retreat, located 500 miles away from
their primary residence in Princeton, New Jersey, was designed to look
like an organic addition to the coastal forest, camouflaged by an exterior
of cedar shingles and an interior of exposed unpainted wood framing.

Encompassing just 648 square feet, the cabin is a rugged refuge with
just one bedroom, one bath, and a wood-burning stove as the sole
source of heat. The exterior walls are not insulated. In fact, they don't
even have drywall or paneling to disguise the framed skeleton or the
pine sheathing that peeks between the naked studs. This allowed the
Chapmans to save on costs *and* achieve a feeling of rustic simplicity that
hearkens back to the carefree days of a summer camp.

In this two-story boat house, the bottom floor is used to store the owners' kayaks, a single rowing
scull and other boating gear. The second story functions as a one-bedroom, one bath retreat.

In the kitchen, the space between the studs proves just wide enough for a paper towel holder. Ann claims that the view of Eggemoggin Reach from the kitchen window makes washing dishes "a pleasure."

Massive stacks of firewood surround the Chapman's tiny cabin, which is heated only by a wood-burning stove. "I like the efficiency of heating with a renewable heating source," Tom Chapman explains.

DESIGNING IN PHASES

"We didn't know how much time we would spend there when we built it," Tom says. But, after purchasing six acres fronting Maine's Eggemoggin Reach and leaving it undeveloped for several years, he and Ann were anxious to "get on the land"—and the water—and start enjoying their investment without sinking all their savings into building a second home. A modest boat house that they could live in, too, seemed like the perfect solution. As a result, the cabin was designed with a hold for the couples' kayaks and Tom's single-rowing scull beneath the main living area.

The structure, designed by architect Bob Knight, of Knight Associates in Blue Hill, Maine, is meant to be finished in phases. Knight designed the structure so that it could serve as a summer escape, yet he ensured that it could be easily winterized one day, either for use as a guesthouse or simply to accommodate the Chapmans if they decide to spend more time there when they retire. Even though the walls are not insulated, "we insulated the foundation and the floor of the sleeping loft over the porch, because that would be tough to do later," explains Knight, who also used insulated glass for the windows and skylights.

The tricky part was making the "unfinished" cabin feel like a welcoming retreat. Knight accomplished this, in part, by calling for the exterior of the frame to be sheathed with pine boards. "Normally that would be plywood, but the boards look better and smell good," he says. "It's an old-fashioned

way of building." The boards were laid on the diagonal to help brace the cabin against the wind, while simultaneously creating an interesting architectural detail that is visible on the interior.

The exposed framework has provided unexpected storage, as well. The spaces between the studs have been put to use as shelves for dishes and glassware in the kitchen and as niches for toiletries in the bathroom. The main living area features one wall lined almost entirely with floor-to-ceiling bookshelves, and now the Chapmans have started utilizing the gaps between the framing as additional storage for board games and tomes on Maine's plants and animals.

"I'm just wondering if books make good insulation," jokes Ann, although the cabin's toasty interior may have more to do with a well-fed wood-burning stove. Tom ensures that the stove never goes hungry, insisting that he finds splitting the trees that fall on his property "therapeutic."

A GLOWING INTERIOR

While the Chapmans originally planned to paint their woodwork white to lighten the walls, Tom says that builder Larry Packwood was so enamored by the look of the natural wood that he called the homeowner and asked to leave it unpainted. "He said, 'It's like being inside a pumpkin,'" Tom recalls. "It glows." The Chapmans are glad they heeded Packwood's advice. "It's taken on an even richer patina since then," Tom says.

The small kitchen features simple open-shelves above the range. "We wanted the kitchen to be uncomplicated, like the rest of the house," Tom says. On the remaining two kitchen walls, windows take precedence over upper shelves or cabinets.

In this tiny coastal cabin, no space is wasted. Bathroom shelves were created by inserting pine boards between the wall studs.

Thanks to its "unfinished" state, without paneling or drywall covering the exterior stud walls, this cabin retains the breezy feel of a summer camp. Low-voltage lights, mounted to the rafters, provide indirect illumination and cast a warm glow upon the vaulted ceiling. "They're like stars," Ann Chapman observes.

Dual lofts on each end of the house provide cozy accommodations for overnight guests. "When everybody is sleeping up in the lofts, it's a little bit like 'The Waltons,'" Ann says about the open loft design. "You hear, 'Good night! Good night! Good night!'"

As it turns out, creating a light, airy interior was not a problem, thanks to plenty of windows and skylights. "It's like being in a tree house, with these wonderful outlooks onto the water and the woods," Tom notes. "I don't nap at home," Ann chimes in, "but up there, I love to lie down on the sofa underneath the skylights and watch the trees and the sky and the clouds go by, and I drift off to sleep."

OFFSHORE EXCURSIONS

Over the years, Ann and Tom have found themselves wanting to spend more and more time at their wooded retreat, which is warm enough to live in from late spring through early autumn. Ann, a teacher, is at liberty to visit throughout the summer, and Tom has installed a home office in one of the two small lofts, enabling him to work remotely for a couple of weeks at a stretch.

At the cabin, he says, "I can find this balance between work and pleasure. If the tide is up and the water is calm, I get up and get the day going with a good row, then come back and do my work." Sometimes, he is accompanied on his early morning excursions by one of the curious seals that hang out on the large rocks just offshore. "I'll look up and see a head come up out of the water with these two gigantic, globelike eyes, and it will be one of the seals," he says.

Other times, he and Ann will paddle their kayaks out together, headed toward one of the islands that lie half a mile offshore. When they're not picnicking on the islands, they often lunch down by the beach, watching the sailboats and the seals, the ospreys and the eider ducks.

A SLOWER PACE OF LIFE

"There's this incredible beauty and connection with nature here," Tom says. "It stimulates our interest in a whole new spectrum of things. Tromping through the woods, we get to know about different flora and fauna that we never would have paid attention to before. We're enveloped by a different pace of life."

"Even when we're not there," Ann says, "it's nice to remember the air and the islands and the light and the sounds. It's something we would like to bottle up and bring home. And we can, through our memories, all winter long."

Loft Living

A loft can be one of the hardest-working spaces in a cabin. Larger than a hallway but less defined than a room, a loft is typically separated from the living space below by a railing, rather than a wall. Its open, amorphous configuration leaves it completely subject to personal interpretation.

Depending on how you furnish it, a loft can become a home office, game room, art studio, library, personal gym, guest sleeping quarters—or all of the above. One cabin owner equipped his upper space with a whirlpool tub.

Beyond a loft's ability to fulfill whatever functional needs your floor plan may not otherwise accommodate, it can also perform double duty as a scenic lookout. For instance, a cabin perched on a mountainside in Old Fort, North Carolina, features a tiny third-floor loft accessible only by a steeply pitched ladder. The loft's sole purpose is to skim the treetops and proffer a bird's-eye view of

North Carolina's shimmering Lake Lure. But it is well worth the climb to reach this aerie above the clouds.

Inspired by a visit to that cabin, one couple added a loft to their own home simply to take advantage of the valley views that are framed by a two-story wall of windows along their cabin's rear wall. Once the loft was built, they discovered that they had room for a trundle bed beneath the sloping tongue-and-groove ceiling, gaining two extra berths. Thus, they gained an unexpectedly practical use for a space that began as nothing more than a "lofty" indulgence.

The staggered ends of hand-peeled Douglas fir logs accentuate the framework in the loft of this family ski escape in Telluride, Colorado. Exercise equipment tucks in neatly beneath the sloped ceiling, while a dormer window provides ample headroom and plenty of light for a remote office.

Bunk beds make the most of limited space (above), and built-in bookshelves do double-duty as a guard rail in a sleeping loft at a writer's retreat (below left). At a timber frame in Vermont, a catwalk leads to an intimate nook housing a whirlpool tub (below right).

A Place to Unplug

Family bonding in a post-and-beam home

:: No telephone. No TV. No video games. No problem! That's exactly the kind of unplugged paradise Joe Johnson had in mind when he and his wife, Jill, began plotting a second-home escape on a 160-acre tract of wetlands and rolling woodlands in Michigan. Their getaway vehicle—an intimate timber frame just big enough to embrace their family of five—abuts the 60,000-acre Pinckney State Recreation Area, and the only sound is the symphony of frogs, punctuated by the soulful soprano of the occasional coyote. It sounds like heaven, right?

But it wasn't idyllic—at least not at first—for the Johnson's three kids. "The children thought we were torturing them, because there is no TV here," Joe recalls with a laugh. "Our six-year-old said, 'you're ruining my life!' I said, 'you'll survive.'"

Vertical cedar tongue-in-groove siding was specially milled for the Johnson's home. Sandstone steps help ground the structure to the site.

Wormy chestnut floors and a white-painted tongue-and-groove ceiling accented by oak beams make the kitchen feel warm and inviting. The "Mr. Ed" door, built by a team of carpenters, is not only charming, it's practical. "Out here, if you leave the door open, something walks in—chipmunks, squirrels, turtles," Joe Johnson explains with a laugh. By opening only the top portion, he can let in the breeze without admitting the wildlife.

THRIVING IN THE WOODS

In fact, his children not only survived, they have thrived, along with their parents, during visits to their post-and-beam home in the woods.

"We've got a big stack of hay bales the kids can climb on," Joe says. "They use a bow and arrow. We've got a BB gun and an old tin can we shoot at, and we have a huge tree fort they hang out in. Every time we go, we come back with something the kids have caught—a snake or a turtle or a frog."

The timber frame home was designed to foster family togetherness. Its massive oak posts and beams, held together by mortise-and-tenon joinery and affixed with kiln-dried oak pegs, lend the home the feel of an old-fashioned farmhouse that has already withstood the test of time. The large living room, which adjoins the country-style dining area and kitchen, has become the Johnsons' favorite communal hangout.

SCALING DOWN TO COZY

The timber frame features soaring cathedral ceilings in the great room, creating a striking sensation of space, yet each room was deliberately scaled to very human proportions. In fact, after viewing the initial blueprints, the Johnsons asked the architects to subtract two feet from every side.

"We said, let's just keep making it smaller," Joe says. "With this house sitting in the middle of the woods, it had to feel really cozy."

Strategically placed windows take advantage of the views and fill the home with light, but the Johnsons were also mindful of what they wanted to keep out. The Dutch-style door (a design reminiscent of the door featured on the television show *Mr. Ed*) in the kitchen, for instance, can be opened at the top to let in the breeze without welcoming in the critters. "There are coyotes out in our front yard," Joe says, "so it's nice to have sturdy doors and windows and walls."

A ROOM WITH A VIEW

One of the family's preferred features is the tower, which is accessed by a spiral staircase leading from the second floor. "That's the place to sit, because you have a 360-degree view, and you can see for more than half a mile," Joe notes. "It's like a tree house." He keeps a pair of binoculars handy to spy on the wildlife—fox, coyote, deer, and birds of all kinds.

"Our kids love it," Joe says of their weekend retreat. "Who knows what they'll be like as teenagers, but for now," he says, "they're perfectly happy."

Multiple window groupings take advantage of the Johnsons' views of surrounding wetlands and woods, but the sturdy oak timbers lend a reassuring sense of strength when coyotes howl outside at night.

A second-floor bedroom is accessed by French doors and overlooks the great room below.

The Johnsons' daughter enjoys a theatrical balcony just off her bedroom. "That's where I give my State of the Union, my State of the Family address," Joe jokes.

Stairways with Style

A stairway can be made more than a physical conveyance. With a little ingenuity, it can be the architectural highlight of your cabin. If you don't have enough room for a continuous run of stairs, you may decide to add a landing or install a space-saving spiral staircase that draws you inexorably upward.

After you nail down the local building code details (tread widths and rises, for example), consider how you might imbue the various parts of your staircase with your specific cabin style.

:: Treads. Half-round log treads are sturdy and casual. Metal treads, by contrast, will add a crisp, contemporary flair.

:: Baluster options. For rustic appeal, you could select straight, small-diameter logs or opt for Adirondack-style twigs and branches. Metal balusters are adaptable and can look elegant or informal, depending on the pattern of the metal work. Or combine these styles by creating twig balusters out of metal for a more contemporary feel.

:: Newel posts. Top a newel post with a whimsical wood carving, or use a knotty tree trunk as a post.

Facing page: One of the most striking features of this home on Martha's Vineyard is its blend of rich, honey-colored wood tones. In order to maintain the site lines throughout this room, the architect designed a circular stairway that seems almost transparent, thanks to the delicate cypress railings and yellow pine treads that feature a stylized support beneath each step, rather than a solid kick-plate. The gnarly Y-shaped oak posts were felled on the owners' property.

This home's ingenious owner/builder constructed his half-log stairs almost entirely from materials found on his property in Arden, North Carolina. Two hickory trees were sawn into stair treads, and the stringers are made of those trees' solid round trunks. The owner individually notched the stringers with a chain saw as he embedded the stair treads. Twigs for the mountain laurel railing were also gathered from his land, but the distinctive newel post and the carving of a bear reading a book are from Jackson Hole.

To access a new master bedroom in the attic, these do-it-yourself homeowners installed a ladder-like stairway using wooden treads and blueberry branches in place of balusters.

A Passion for Preservation

A beach cabin emerges from the rubble of what seemed unsalvageable

:: Not many folks would have regarded the tiny 150-year-old pine barn on Cape Cod as a cozy hideaway where they would want to spend the rest of their lives. But looking beyond the wavy wooden plank floor, the boarded-up windows, and the supporting posts weakened by insects and humidity, Bob and Barbara Nickerson saw what others did not—the potential for a great beach cabin where they could eventually retire.

Though the old barn was nearly beyond repair, it was located almost within sight of the surf. "It's only six houses from the beach, and you can't beat that," Bob says. "Barbara and I are both really outdoor people—not city people," he explains.

Once a candidate for a tear-down, this old barn now serves as a cozy coastal retreat.

KEEPING HISTORY ALIVE

Bob also loved the barn's timber-frame skeleton—and the history behind it. His parents had owned the barn since 1963, and his family had lived in the house next door for almost 200 years. Bob imagined that his great-great-grandfather had played beside it as a boy, and he himself remembered climbing into the barn's dual lofts and nearly falling through the rotted floor while visiting his grandparents. Later, his family would use the barn-cum-cabin as a warm-weather retreat, but it was never outfitted with plumbing or electricity and had badly deteriorated by the time Bob's parents were ready to sell it in 1996.

Fortunately, Barbara shares her husband's passion for old structures and supported his plan to repair the barn. "We're not into 'new,'" explains Barbara. "We both prefer to preserve older things that are worthwhile."

After asking a timber framer to confirm that the barn could indeed be saved, the Nickersons contacted a general contractor whose father had been best friends with Bob's dad. "I think he thought we were a little crazy at first, restoring this old barn," Bob admits. But the Nickersons could not be swayed. "We wanted to maintain the barn aspect of it," Bob says, "and we wanted to keep as much of the wood inside as we could."

HANDLING SPACE LIMITATIONS

The Nickersons knew that the barn, which encompasses only about 1,000 square feet, would not be spacious enough to accommodate them when they eventually move there full-time from their home in Texas. So, after poring over dozens of magazines and books in search of ideas, they sketched out an addition that architect Sarah Jane Porter used as the basis for an initial set of blueprints.

The new timber-frame addition would attach to the barn with a simple shed roof in the back (where the new kitchen and dining area would be located) and a hip roof on the side (where the master suite and a second bathroom with a washer/dryer would be situated). The barn itself would serve as the den, with the loft space pressed into service as guest bedrooms.

In keeping with the cabin's history, the home features French doors which can be shuttered over with sliding barn doors. During renovations, the structure was wrapped with structural insulated panels and then sheathed with new cedar shingles and clapboard siding.

An overhead loft creates an intimate space below for the sitting room. The old barn, which is made mostly of Eastern White pine, required extensive renovations, but the owners saved as many of the original posts and beams as possible.

"When you're in the kitchen, you have a view of everything, which makes it feel much bigger," says Bob. "We like to cook, so when you're in there, you're still a part of other activities." Shell-patterned café curtains offer a nod to the beach, which is just six blocks away.

The general contractor brought in a consultant who had traveled throughout Europe studying post-and-beam cathedrals, barns, and houses dating back to the fourteenth century. These structures, which have survived six or seven hundred years, offer builders today excellent models for construction methods that are bound to last.

REPAIRING THE DAMAGE

This kind of knowledge about historic timber frames informed the Nickerson project, which required extensive renovation. One of the first things that had to be done was lifting the entire barn up a few inches off its foundation, ratcheting it up with cast-iron screw jacks one-sixteenth of an inch at a time. This was necessary to replace the rotted sill plate and install a new subfloor. (The original plank flooring, unfortunately, was too rotted to be saved and was eventually replaced with random-width oak planks.) The project crew also dug two feet under the foundation to install new footings around the perimeter.

Meanwhile, workers removed the majority of the wallboards in order to repair the lower portion of the support posts, which had been damaged by powder-post beetles and moisture. They numbered the boards, so that after they fixed the posts, they could nail them back in the same place.

Posts salvaged from an old mill in western Massachusetts were added to support the additional roof load of the new addition. Because of the age of the posts, they blended right in with the original barn.

After the recycled posts were erected and the wallboards were nailed back in their original positions, the restored barn was lowered onto a new plywood deck. The work crew then dug out a full cellar for the addition, poured the foundation walls, and installed the subfloor.

THE NEW BARN RAISING

Finally, it was time for the workers to erect the new pine timber frame. Bob and Barbara, who flew in from Texas to visit the site at least once a month, helped hold the walls as the crew fastened the timbers with one-inch oak pegs, some of which the Nickersons had carved themselves. Both the old and new sections were enclosed with structural insulated panels, and workers added several new windows, four skylights, and two sets of self-supporting oak stairs leading up to the old lofts.

The Nickersons applied the finishing touches themselves, painting the trim and staining the exterior clapboards and shingles. By March 1998, six months after they began the restoration, the home was complete.

For Barbara, the reward was well worth all the hard work. "We would do it again in a heartbeat," she says. In fact, Barbara and Bob are already searching for another old barn, which they plan to connect to their new kitchen and use as a dining room.

Next time, they hope to play an even more active role in the restoration. "We enjoy that, working side by side, and the physical labor," Barbara explains. "You have to have the right character for it—and the right marriage!"

A loft, converted into a guest bedroom, is illuminated by a large bank of windows, as well as skylights overhead. While the Nickersons were keen to maintain the appearance of a barn, which would typically have few, if any, windows, they ultimately deemed the additional windows and skylights worthy updates. "It gets so dark for so long in the winter," Barbara says. "We had to come to a comfortable compromise within ourselves."

When renovating this 19th-century barn on Cape Cod, the owners created a simple, open floor plan.

An Original Riverside Homestead

A couple breathes new life into a forgotten cabin

:: Nestled in a verdant valley in northwestern Montana, a cozy cabin hugs the banks of the Swan River. Inside, honey-colored tongue-and-groove paneling and low, wood-beamed ceilings welcome guests like a warm embrace. Outside, horses graze in a pasture sheltered by the mountains, and a weathered old barn nearby recalls a long-ago era when pioneers first put down roots west of the Rockies.

The peaceful, swaying grasses of the flatlands caught the eye of Michael and Sherry O'Hearn, a Florida couple whose second home clung to the mountainside above. They would drive by everyday, recalls Sherri, a soft-spoken native Texan, and "right in front of us was this beautiful pasture where they were haying on one side, and they kept horses on the other. We thought, isn't that lovely, with the view of the Jewell Basin Hiking Area. We just always admired the tranquillity of the spot."

Duck decoys, displayed in glass-fronted antique bookcases, and a collection of old fishing creels hung on the cabin walls serve as useful reminders of its proximity to the Swan River.

A FOUND FARMSTEAD

Yet buying the cabin and its ranch property was the farthest thing from their minds in the summer of 2000. At first, the couple inquired about renting the property on behalf of Sherry's brother. When the original owner decided to sell the house instead of renting it, her brother backed away from the idea. But Sherry recognized the value of the property, which was an original Montana homestead. "I told my brother, 'You've got to buy this! These properties don't come up very often.' He wasn't quite ready to do it, so we decided that we would do it to keep it in the family," she explains.

"You could do all the things on the flat piece of property that you couldn't do up on the mountain," Sherry continues. "The mountain gives you a vista that would knock your socks off, but down there, we could keep little farm animals. We could sow hay. We could be urban farmers, if you will," she says with a laugh. "We also love kayaking and fishing, and we thought, wouldn't that be a wonderful location?"

The O'Hearns realized that restoring the 3,072-square-foot home would require considerable effort. Though the house was less than 20 years old and was structurally sound, the lodgepole pine D-logs had yellowed and needed to be sanded and restained. The countertops in the kitchen and bathrooms needed to be replaced, as did the outdated appliances. The existing stone fireplace, which covered an entire wall, would have to go, and the bare-bones basement, with its concrete floor and plywood walls, begged for a little warmth.

CREATING AN INTIMATE SCALE

The couple hired the contractor who had remodeled their main Montana home. Their goal was to retain the warmth of the original scale. The homeowners considered removing the roof and vaulting the structure, but Sherry ultimately nixed that idea. "In my opinion, this was a little jewel box," she says. "To have vaulted the ceilings would not have been appropriate, since that was not the way it was made. Why not bring it back to its original state?"

As part of the ranch renovation, the O'Hearns added one thousand square feet of deck, including a new covered entry porch. Oversized log posts and log railings create the feel of an old turn-of-the-century homestead.

The owners refinished the kitchen cabinets and replaced the original laminate counters with custom-made wooden slabs. New windows in the breakfast nook offer a 180 degree view of the Swan River.

UPDATING THE OUTDATED

One of the most important steps was removing the yellowed varnish. An extensive crew, which included the O'Hearns' dedicated housekeeper, used orbital sanders on every inch of wood, inside and out, to prepare it for a new coat of stain. "That took days and days, but when we got done, it was worth every minute, because the rich tone of the new stain just looks fabulous," comments the contractor, who notes that Sherry painstakingly experimented with the stain until she achieved the custom-blended golden color she desired.

The O'Hearns replaced the house's old, inefficient windows with larger, double-paned windows. The shutters, which feature evergreen cutouts designed by Sherry, are coated with a custom paint blended to match the exterior aluminum-cladding of the new windows.

The exterior renovation also called for tripling the deck space and installing a covered porch supported by ten-inch log porch posts. "They're fat for the scale of the building, but it just makes it feel more substantial and massive," says the contractor, who added log railings around the new 1,000-square-foot deck, as well.

A WOOD-CLAD INTERIOR

Wood accents prevailed on the interior, too. Wide-planked rustic fir floors, milled to match the original in the living room, were installed in the bedrooms and the basement. The walls and ceiling of the bathrooms and basement were covered with tongue-and-groove paneling, which was also custom-milled to match the existing woodwork in other parts of the home. The woodwork is unusual for its rounded edges; instead of the tongue-and-groove butting right next to each other, there's a flat space between.

Three-inch thick slabs of ponderosa pine, secured from the same mill as the tongue-and-groove paneling and fir floors, form one-of-a-kind countertops in the bathrooms and in the kitchen. The kitchen received a new apron-front sink and updated appliances as well.

The addition of wooden ceiling beams in the kitchen, dining room, and living room further enhance the home's woodsy lodge effect.

The homeowners also utilized surplus materials from another project, the construction of a guesthouse for their second home. When they tore down the old fireplace in the cabin, for instance, they replaced it with local Chief Cliff stone that they had on hand after completing the fireplace in the guesthouse. Likewise, they salvaged bits of tumbled marble left over from the bathrooms in the mountaintop guesthouse and used them for the bathroom floors and showers at

the cabin. "It was like throwing puzzle pieces on the floor, and you worked with whatever came out," says Sherry, who enjoyed the mosaic effect.

HONING A HOMESTEAD DECOR

Her uncanny abilities to mix and match long-forgotten treasures are evidenced throughout the warm, inviting home, which she decorated herself. In the living/dining area, for example, Pennsylvania Dutch paddles used

Vintage creels and fishing nets, as well as paddles, are part of the homeowner's collection of fishing gear.

for removing loaves of bread from wood-fired ovens hang alongside South American canoe paddles, which the O'Hearns acquired in exchange for a few pairs of Nike tennis shoes during a trip down the Amazon River. Another canoe paddle, retrieved from the Swan River and bent by the current, creates an eye-catching arch atop a doorway. On the other side of the doorway, Sherry has created a vignette from antique fishing tackle—yet another reminder of the river that flows just beyond the front door.

She ferreted out many of the antiques and accessories that fill the house at "trash and treasure" shops all over Montana, searching for pieces evocative of an old riverside homestead. She combined these with comfortable custom-made furnishings, like a gray-and-green leather sofa, and family heirlooms, such as her grandmother's weathered trunk, which has found pride of place in the living room.

In fact, Sherry says, her Mexican grandmother's presence can be felt throughout the house, which is adorned with Southwestern-style rugs and rich raspberry, jade, and aqua hues. "You know, she always had such style, and my mother had it, too," she says. "They helped me to appreciate color and scale. I think that's a real gift they gave me, if indeed I have it," she adds modestly.

If her grandmother were alive to enjoy the revamped cabin today, "I think she would love it," Sherry says with an affectionate laugh. "I think she would be happy that her pieces had traveled so far and were still resting in a very happy home."

In the bedroom, as in the den, the homeowners combine vertical tongue-and-groove paneling with the horizontal lines created by the log courses, breaking up the monotone hue of the wood. A triangular-shaped cupboard, which nestles tightly into a corner, and swing arm lamps, which don't need to rest on end tables, save space and make the room feel larger.

The bunk room can accommodate multiple overnight guests.

The bathroom, once sheathed in non-descript drywall, received a rustic makeover, with custom-milled paneling, a wooden counter, and a distinctive bridle-and-horseshoe mirror. Hand towels embroidered with the ranch insignia hang on a matching horseshoe-accented rack.

Storing Sports Equipment

One of the primary reasons we find ourselves attracted to cabin life is the opportunity to get closer to the activities we enjoy, whether that is hunting, fishing, kayaking, or schussing down powder-white slopes. But the more passionate you are about sports, the more gear you need. So where do you stow it all in a cabin?

One possibility is a dedicated storage area, such as a shed or a mudroom. Useful features for these kinds of spaces include:

:: Durable flooring. A stone, tile, or concrete floor that can stand up to dirt and snow.

:: Hooks. Use hooks on the walls and ceiling for hanging dripping-wet waders and bathing suits, vests, helmets, ski poles, oars, or even mountain bikes.

:: Storage for small things. Install small drawers for items such as gloves, hats, and fishing lures.

:: Ventilation. Ventilated shelving is ideal to help gear dry quickly.

:: A place to sit. Entryway benches are practical and welcoming. A slatted cedar chest provides a place to sit and allows air to circulate around boots stored inside.

:: Appropriate security. You may be in the wilderness, but consider installing locks for expensive fishing rods and other valuable equipment.

You can also create storage space both above and below an outdoor deck. Build hinge-top seating benches and place them along a deck's perimeter to hold oars or ski poles and install doors in the skirting material under-neath your deck for a handy place to store water toys and camping gear.

All gun owners know that a safe or cabinets that lock are a must for guns and ammunition, which frequently must be stored separately.

Finally, in a cabin, you always have the option of hiding your gear in plain sight. With your canoe or kayak literally hanging over your head, chances are you'll be inspired to head into the wild more often to explore the great outdoors.

Facing page: On this Colorado ranch, a mudroom is essential. The sturdy brick floor is impervious to mud and snow, and plenty of hooks provide a place to hang cowboy hats, chaps, bridles, coats, and even an old canteen. Boots are conveniently lined up beneath benches, providing a place to sit and change shoes before heading out for a ride.

Right: Though this once river-worthy canoe has been retired to decorative status, it serves as an inspiration to get out and explore nearby Fontana Lake, which is adjacent to the Great Smoky Mountains National Park. Sixteen-foot-high ceilings provide ample display space, and the 10-inch-round northern white pine logs act as a rustic backdrop.

Building a Cabin from Scratch

A pioneering family creates a retreat using their land's natural resources

:: When most kids were still playing with Lincoln Logs, Ken Mattson was already erecting real log structures on his family's farm in northern Indiana and playing with his siblings in a 250-year-old log cabin next to their childhood home. But the true test of Ken's lifelong love of cabins was building a family home with his own hands in the remote North Woods of Wisconsin.

Ken was living in Florida with his wife, Tonja, and their sons, Ricky and Noah, when they decided to stop dreaming and start building. "We always liked the country life, so we started looking around for property," Ken says. When he decided it was time to "move to the country," Ken opened a map of Wisconsin and chose Fifield, population 351. "It's the barest spot on the map, the absolute farthest from any major city you can be," Ken says of the area, which is more heavily populated by timber wolves, black bear, and deer than by humans.

In warmer weather, the porch is a favorite perch for bird watching. In the winter, it keeps firewood dry and serves as a staging area for outdoor pursuits.

USING THE LOCAL MATERIAL

The Mattsons searched around Fifield until they found 40 densely forested acres with a pond and a swamp filled with tamarack trees. That was important, because Ken had already decided that he wanted to build his log home entirely from materials found on his own property, and tamarack was his tree of choice. "Tamarack resembles cypress, yet it sheds its needles, and that makes it a hardwood," he explains. "They never rot, so it's an excellent tree to make a log home with."

Having selected their home site, the Mattsons sold everything they had and moved to Wisconsin in a Winnebago. For a year, Ken put his remodeling business on the back burner so that he could concentrate on building his family's own home. "I didn't have a

In the great room, the wood stove is surrounded by green granite deposited by glaciers 10,000 years ago. The Mattsons collected the stones from their property and from an adjoining parcel. A solid cherry mantel displays a collection of Indian busts, kerosene lamps, and a small model of a canoe.

real job," explains Ken, who lived with his family on-site in the Winnebago. "I just worked and worked on the house, from daylight until dark, for about 15 or 16 hours a day."

A FAMILY AFFAIR

With a lot of help from his boys, then 13 and 11, Ken felled 158 tamaracks in the spring of 1995. "You pick the straight trees and fell them with a chain saw," he says. Afterwards, they peeled them in the swamp with a spud bar and left them to dry.

Six months later, after a generous neighbor cleared the building site with his bulldozer, the Mattsons began retrieving the logs from the swamp. They dragged them out one at a time with a 200-foot rope attached to a four-wheel-drive vehicle driven by Tonja, transporting them a quarter of a mile to the home site. Then they individually scribed and stacked each log and secured every course with 20-inch-long steel pins.

"I remember working one day for 16 hours just setting one log," Ken says. "It was 33 feet long, and I had to drag it out, winch it, and get some block and tackle to pull it up and set it."

As the family worked, they familiarized themselves with the North Woods natives, who stopped by to welcome them, each in their own way. Ken remembers counting as many as 14 deer grazing placidly in a clearing one day, and he recalls the many mornings he sipped his coffee while chickadees serenaded him from their bird feeder. Other visitors were decidedly less friendly. "When we were living in the Winnebago, a

"I like openness," says Ken, who designed and built his log cabin himself. In the great room, the ceilings soar to 17 feet, 9 inches and feature basswood tongue-and-groove paneling, which was harvested from the Mattson's 40-acre spread.

Ken fashioned the stairway's distinctive balusters from cedar trees which grew beside an outhouse that serviced the family before their log cabin was completed. He was inspired when his flashlight beam played over their limb-like arms during a fortuitous late-night jaunt.

black bear and her two cubs ripped our laundry off the line and shredded my flannel shirts," he says ruefully.

As anxious as they were to enclose the home, the Mattsons were unable to install the tin roof, which is supported by black spruce log rafters, before the onset of the harsh Wisconsin winter. "I actually put the roof on in January in the snow," Ken says with a laugh. "I shoveled snow out of the living room through the picture window."

Since the logs were still relatively green, the Mattsons allowed them to settle for a year before chinking, a nine-week process that would have taken even longer without help from Ken's relatives. "My mom took her pointer finger and smeared all the chinking, which is over a mile. She actually wore the fingerprints right off her finger!" Ken says.

A dining table adjacent to the kitchen provides just enough space for Ken and Tonja and their three children, Ricky, Noah, and Kandis, who was born while the home was under construction.

Ken crafted the kitchen cabinets from pines he felled on his own land. It took four people to set into place a black spruce beam, which supports the ceiling. The tiled counters, which match the tile on the floors, are durable and easy to clean.

LIVING OFF THE LAND

To further insulate the home, Ken built 2-foot by 4-foot interior walls lined with R19 insulation, which he also installed in the floor. "You could heat the house with a candle," he insists, though he actually chose to heat it with the sun. Modular solar panels gather power, which is stored in batteries. The stove and hot water heater are gas-powered, and a glass-front, wood-burning stove in the living room also helps keep the home toasty warm in the frigid winters.

Green granite, much of which was gathered from the Mattsons' own property, surrounds the stove. All of the wood trim, including the cherry mantel, the pine cabinetry, the white cedar handrails, and the basswood tongue-and-groove ceiling in the great room, came from the Mattsons' 40 acres as well.

In the autumn of 1999, the Mattsons were finally ready to move in. At first, Ken admits, "I felt like I was going to a place of work, because we had worked so hard to build it. But after a few weeks, it became home." In the winter, he says, "You look out the window and you see the deer, and the snow's coming down and the fire is sparkling. It's just fantastic."

But the greatest satisfaction, perhaps, lies in knowing that he and his family built their home from the ground up, using the bounty of the Great North Woods. As Ken himself notes, "You can't get anymore 'scratch' than that!"

The master bedroom showcases the tamarack logs, which average eight inches in diameter, though some specimens range up to 14 inches. An additional three bedrooms for the children are located on the second floor.

Selecting a Wood Stove

Wood stoves are cabin icons, but today, they can vary greatly in appearance, from basic black to cheerful cherry-red and sleek, futuristic cylinders. Despite the diversity of facades, however, there are just three basic types.

:: **Box stove.** A box stove is perhaps the most elementary version of a wood stove. It draws air through its door, does not seal completely, and has no damper to regulate air intake. These are typically the least expensive wood stoves on the market.

:: **Airtight stove.** The second type, an airtight stove, is just what its name implies—a sealed firebox with a tight-fitting door. A damper, which may be controlled manually or by a thermostat, depending on the model, allows you to adjust air intake, thus controlling how quickly the wood burns.

:: **Pellet stove.** The most recent innovation is the pellet stove. This new kid on the block burns wood-composite pellets, which are fed electronically into the stove's combustion chamber at intervals which are regulated by a timer and a sensor.

Wood stoves can have either solid doors, which radiate more heat, or tempered glass doors, which don't provide as much heat but allow you to enjoy the flickering flames. In either case, a wood stove heats more efficiently than a typical open fireplace, and some stoves can even be rigged up to a heat pump to circulate warm air throughout the house.

Left: A wood stove, raised upon a brick hearth, keeps this master bedroom in Littleton, New Hampshire warm even in cold New England winters. The glass door allows the owners to enjoy the flames from their bed, which is tucked into an alcove beneath a loft that serves as a reading room and office.

Lower left: A sleek Danish wood-burning stove complements this beach retreat's minimalist aesthetic and supplements the warmth provided by the home's passive-solar design. Vermont slate flooring, laid atop six inches of concrete, absorbs heat during the day and radiates it back in the evenings.

Lower right: A substantial manufactured stone surround adds weight and importance to the wood-burning stove, transforming it from a utilitarian object into a focal point for family gatherings. The semicircular hearth is just the right height to serve as a bench, doubling the room's seating capacity.

Facing page: Removable glass windows and an old-style wood stove—which has been converted to gas—keeps this porch warm even in Crested Butte's harsh winters.

Designing a Hearth

When designing a hearth for your cabin, one of the primary considerations is its location. The great room is an obvious choice, but arrange the fireplace against a wall where it will not compete with postcard panoramic views. Locate it in a corner or on a side wall, or position a pass-through firebox in the center of the room. By dividing a casual seating area from the dining room, you can enjoy the flames from two vantage points. Other possible locations include the kitchen, master bedroom, and master bath.

Once you find a place for your hearth, you must consider the materials you wish to use and the style you'd like to achieve.

:: Firebox surrounds. Think about the material that will surround the firebox. Stone, whether natural or one of the realistic man-made varieties, complements any cabin. Depending on the type of stone and how it's stacked, the hearth can look either rustic or refined. Other traditional choices for firebox surrounds include brick, wood, and tile.

:: Mull over the mantel. A chunky slab of stone speaks of durability and permanence, while a half-log shelf is homey and humble. The corbels that support the mantel can be stone, logs, or carved pieces of wood.

Ultimately, one of the most important decisions regarding your hearth is whether to install a wood-burning fireplace or a gas log unit. If you want flames to appear at the flick of a switch, then it's got to be gas. But if you pine for the authentic, earthy scent of smoke, then wood is the way to go.

Facing page: This guest room in the Adirondack Mountains features a pass-through fireplace that separates the sitting room and bedroom. A starburst pattern formed with rustic logs abuts the chimney's cultured stone veneer, drawing attention to the cathedral ceiling.

Left: A sandstone fireplace serves as the heart of this two-room cabin on the Uncompahgre River in Colorado. Besides the fireplace, the only light is provided by a hand-forged candle chandelier and kerosene lamps.

Below: In South Carolina, an outdoor fireplace combining salvaged red bricks with a mantel and corbels fashioned from 100-year-old hand-peeled cypress afford this new log home the feel of the old South.

A Lakeside Escape

Riding out stormy weather to forge a refuge by the shore

:: What happens when a mountain man meets a beach and boat kind of girl? Can they find a vacation home that allows them both to live happily ever after? That was the challenge faced by Eric and Jen Flo of Seattle, Washington. "Eric grew up hiking and climbing," Jen says. "I grew up with the dock and the boat."

Fortunately, Eric and Jen both like to camp, and it was one of those excursions that initially led them to Lake Cushman on the Olympic Peninsula in Seattle. "We took our mothers out camping for Mother's Day," Eric recalls. "The place we wanted to go was snowed in, so the Forest Service Ranger recommended Lake Cushman. It was a beautiful blue-sky weekend, and we thought, 'Wow! This is gorgeous! We would love to have a place out here.'"

A purlin style timber frame system is one of the stronger methods of building. It features two ridge beams which support the 18-foot-high great room cathedral ceiling. The area experiences high snow loads and powerful winds.

MAKING THE DECISION TO BUY

Cut to February of the following year. Eric was shivering in the pouring rain, slogging through a muddy lakeside lot that was up for sale. The wedge-shaped parcel was only 15 feet wide at the curb. Tiny streams that sprung up in the rain crisscrossed the property, and the lot was littered with debris because the community had used the long-empty area as a dumping ground. Yet this half-acre, triangular plot boasted 180 feet of scenic lake frontage and an incomparable view of the majestic Olympic Mountains. The difficulty of deciding whether or not to buy was compounded by the fact that Jen had been unable to

accompany him, and Eric had to make up his mind right then and there.

"I stood there for two hours and hemmed and hawed and tried to imagine what it would look like when the lake was full and the sky was blue," Eric recalls. "Finally, I said, 'Let's go for it.'" Fortunately, when Jen saw the property, she approved of Eric's choice.

This cabin's frame is Douglas Fir, which is known for its minimal checking, strength, and stability. The couple appreciated the fact that the timber was not logged, but was blown down by the wind. "It was a chance to recycle, which was great," Eric explains. The great room drops down one foot from the kitchen in order to accommodate the natural slope of the land.

The sleek lines of the maple cabinets echo the clean, simple design of a cherry table and benches, which were crafted by the Pennsylvania Amish. The Flos chose to use benches, rather than chairs, to flank the length of the table in order to maintain an unobstructed view out of French doors which open onto an expansive deck. A stainless steel oven hood reflects the gray tones of the counters and Italian slate-colored floor tiles.

"He walked me through the lot, and when we got to the view, the first thing I said was, 'Yes, you did it right!'" she laughs.

"We started out saying, 'We're just going to go camp there,'" Eric recalls. But a visit to a timber-frame lodge on a ski trip to Mount Hood changed their minds, convincing them to build their own post-and-beam house by the water. "With our view of the mountains and lake, we needed a house that had some weight to it to bring in the grandeur of the Great Northwest," Jen explains. "We wanted a lodge feel," Eric adds. "That was our goal."

CAMPING OUT

A tour of the Seattle Home Show, where they spotted an oversized photo of a house plan that would highlight their mountain views, confirmed their decision to build a timber frame home. "We saw that great big window, those big tall posts going up and the high purlins, and we said, 'Wow, that's impressive. That is the one!'" Eric recalls.

"We will spend forever looking for something until we see exactly what we want," Jen explains. "When we see it, that's it!"

The couple became deeply involved with the construction process, and Eric even camped out on-site as the contractor's team erected the structure. "I was just a grunt," he admits. "I went and got nails, and I held up posts and I stuck things together. But I can look at some of the purlins in the great room and remember, it was a windy, cold miserable day and it was about to

rain when we put those up. We used a crane to put the rafters in, but the frame went up by hand. You can think back to those stories."

Within a week, the frame was complete. Then the bottom dropped out of the sky.

BATTLING THE ELEMENTS

It rained for 121 consecutive days, while the work crew gamely carried on beneath a shelter of giant tarps that quickly became tattered by gusting winds. First, they installed the pre-oiled, 2-by-8 pine tongue-and-groove paneling. Then they wrapped the house with a 6-millimeter plastic vapor barrier and 4 inches of rigid foam, which was strapped down by 1-by-4 battens. Next they affixed prestained clear vertical grain cedar siding to the battens and tackled the

Jen and Eric Flo modified an existing floor plan to accommodate a first-floor master bedroom. Now the master bedroom has access to a wraparound deck and offers spectacular views of the mountains across the lake.

Skylights and adjustable track lighting illuminate the loft. Eastern white pine tongue-and-groove paneling provides an attractive contrast to the darker, honey-colored fir timber frame.

standing seam metal roof, which was only half finished when the snows came. Roof adhesives can't be applied unless the roof is dry, so what should have taken three days turned into three weeks.

At last, the skies cleared, and cultured stone accents were applied to the exterior of the chimney and the base of the house, anchoring the structure to a low-maintenance landscape specially created for the site. Weathered logs and long grasses gave the sandy septic field a beach feeling that fit in well with the lakeside surroundings, and large stones were used to create a natural-looking bulkhead along the shore.

The Flos made a few changes to the blueprints to accommodate their lot and their lifestyle, as well. The narrow width of the building site required that they install a front-entry "garage and a half" that was still long enough to park their boat, rather than the two-car side entry garage originally planned.

MAKING WAY FOR KIDS

The couple also opted to move the master bedroom to the first floor and to relocate tiled areas such as the laundry room and powder room so that they were easily accessible from the kitchen. "There is a sliding glass door in the kitchen, which is the main entrance from the lake," Jen explains. "So now, you can walk in that sliding glass door, dripping wet and covered in sand or mud, and get to all the necessities without having to set foot on the carpet. That was a big thing, knowing that we would have lots of company and kids running in and out all day," says Jen, who discovered while building that she was pregnant with twins Michael and Sean.

Almost nine months after breaking ground, the Flo family's 2,650-square-foot, three-bedroom, two-and-a-half bath vacation home was complete. "Eventually, we would like to retire there," Jen says. But for now, she adds, "It's a great little getaway, a place to grow up and make memories for our boys."

Sliding glass doors from the kitchen/dining area and the master bedroom provide ready access to the deck. A pathway defined by paving stones leads towards the lake.

A Cabin with Character

A small log home by a river fulfills big fly-fishing dreams

:: Bigger isn't always better, as Jim and Karen Grace learned when they built a snug little log cabin in Montana. Sometimes, supersized dreams come wrapped up in small packages.

Everything about their Western retreat is modest in scale. Jim, a former marketing and advertising executive who jokingly describes himself as "a frustrated architect," designed the 1,188-square-foot pine cabin. It sits on a heavily wooded three-acre lot alongside a swift-running river near the tiny town of Red Lodge, which boasts an equally tidy population of just 2,300.

For the Graces, who discovered the town 30 years ago while on a ski trip, the cabin is the perfect place to escape the stress of their working life in Florida and plan for the day they'll finally retire in Red Lodge. But it's a much cozier haven than they originally imagined.

The Grace's log home is only 80 yards from Rock Creek, where Jim loves to fly fish. The Grace's collection of fly-fishing equipment includes a vintage creel and bamboo rod. Their flies, such as the hair-wing royal coachman, are ready to use at any time.

The galley-style kitchen isn't large, but custom-made hickory cabinets and a bar topped by a character log and faced with stone lend it plenty of character. A skylight—one of two in the kitchen—helps prevent the home from seeming dark, despite the fact that it is surrounded by trees.

"I've never had a house that didn't have separate rooms for everything," says Karen, who likes the fact that the action is centered around the great room. The 14-foot cathedral ceiling and large windows make the room feel more spacious and bring the outside in. A deer skin hanging over the mantel disguises the television. To the left of the fireplace, a chair made from an oxcart from Vietnam serves as a hat rack.

MAKING LOCATION A PRIORITY

When Jim and Karen first started planning their get-away several years ago, they envisioned a grand lodge presiding over at least 20 acres nestled beside the river and surrounded by the forest, with a breathtaking panoramic view. "What we quickly learned is that some of those things are mutually exclusive," Karen says. "We couldn't have a fabulous mountain view and trees all around, for instance. So we ended up making choices."

Their first decision was to make location, rather than lot size, their priority. As long as it was close to the river, where Jim could indulge his passion for fly-fishing, a house on a smaller, wooded lot would do just fine. "When you have trees all around, you feel like you have a lot of space, whether or not you literally do," Karen explains.

Whittling down the big dream home Jim had already designed proved equally practical. "I realized it would be years before I can afford to build that house," Jim says. "Finally, it dawned on me to build a guesthouse. I thought we could stay in that for a few years, and I could cut the size of the main house which would be built later."

SMALL, YET VIBRANT

Jim, who honed his design skills while renovating a number of houses over the years, quickly dashed off a new set of drawings for the guesthouse. These plans called for a one-level cabin with two bedrooms, a great room that combines a galley-style kitchen with a living/dining area, and a screened-in patio that does double duty as additional dining space and as a sunlit studio where Jim can paint. An innovative bathroom design features a private water closet and separate sink connecting to each bedroom, with a shower/laundry room located in between.

With Jim's plans in hand, things moved quickly. The Graces had already decided on a builder who was redoing a house right next to the house they were

renting, and a log home company converted Jim's graph-paper designs into log home blueprints. By April 2004—six months after breaking ground—the house was complete.

Jim made a concerted effort to pack as much punch per square inch as he could. His contractor helped him secure a pair of character logs, one of which serves as the ridge beam in the great room. The other was used as a mantel for a large stone fireplace, with the remainder forming the top of a bar that separates the kitchen from the living area.

Sandstone floors, warmed by radiant heating, form a solid base for the great room, and the stone slabs face the kitchen bar. Outside, details such as Adirondack-style twig railings and a carving of a moose on the front door lend the home a woodsy charm.

The Graces still plan to build a "main house"—also designed by Jim—but they hope to maintain the same cozy feeling they've captured so well in their guesthouse. As Karen observes, "It's almost like a cocoon—very comforting and secure. I've discovered that I really like small!"

Two bicycles stand at the ready beside the front door, should the Graces decide to pedal into Red Lodge for the afternoon. As an homage to the massive moose which the Graces have encountered on their property, the front door features a carving of a moose and a cheeky sign above that reads "Moose Drop-In."

Jim's fly-fishing gear hangs neatly on the wall outside the screened porch. Just inside, he keeps a couple of aluminum pots, which he bangs together to scare away bear when they appear at his door.

Facing page: The screened-in porch, which connects to both the master bedroom and the great room, expands the Grace's living space year round, thanks to removable Plexiglas storm windows that fit over the screens and radiant heating beneath the stone floors. Jim, who learned to paint horses from a Crow Indian in Red Lodge, sometimes uses the space as an artist's studio.

Planning Outdoor Rooms

When adding a porch, patio, or deck to your cabin, there are several key points to bear in mind. How do you plan to use it? Where do you want to site it? What is the local climate?

If you expect many visitors at your cabin, and you like to entertain outside, you will obviously require a larger outdoor room than you would if you only want to savor the sunrise with a cup of coffee or recline in a hammock. To comfortably accommodate dining space for four requires an area that measures 12 feet by 12 feet, while a free-standing hammock needs an area about 9 feet long and 6 feet wide.

When deciding where to site your outdoor space, think about your views, the path of the sun, and the prevailing winds. If you overlook a lake or the mountains, taking ad-

vantage of the view will likely be your primary consideration. Otherwise, keep in mind that a north-facing orientation is cool, while south-facing is generally warm and sunny. If strong winds or the heat of the sun interfere with how you would ideally like to locate your porch, patio, or deck, consider planting trees and bushes, or adding latticework walls and angled rafters overhead to shield you from the elements. Flowering plants and trailing vines will contribute to the space's visual appeal, as well.

Next, consider the climate. If the mosquitoes at your cabin are bigger than vultures and twice as vicious, a screened-in porch may be your best bet. In colder climes, think about adding an outdoor fireplace or installing radiant heating beneath a stone floor.

Facing page: A gracious, 700-square-foot deck allows plenty of room for lounging in a hammock, dining al fresco, or catching some rays in a fleet of Adirondack chairs while taking in the view of Montana's Whitefish Range. The timber-framed shelter, constructed of reclaimed Douglas Fir posts and beams with a tongue-and-groove pine soffit, echoes the home's timber accents.

Left: Stretching 24 feet long, a wide, welcoming front porch allows the owners of this Nordic pine cabin in Jackson Hole, Wyoming, to enjoy panoramic views of the slopes. Stone columns, topped by gently tapered posts, lend architectural interest to the log façade.

Below: When the owners of this cabin moved to middle Tennessee, they brought with them a fireplace mantel from their former home in southern Louisiana. Crafted from reclaimed cypress by the wife's father, this sentimental mantel now takes pride of place on the front porch, outfitted with antique brass and glass doorknobs where the family can hang their coats.

Useful Outbuildings

The reasons for errecting an outbuilding are as varied as their appearance. They can maintain the architectural integrity of your cabin and keep it from seeming too large and unwieldy by outsourcing functions, such as guest quarters or a workshop. Second, outbuildings enable you to take full advantage of more remote parts of your property. If you find yourself continually drawn to a favorite location, for instance, a permanent shelter will help protect you from the elements and encourage you to enjoy it throughout the year. Finally, these structures can simply answer a practical need, such as providing a barn for your horses or a cozy kennel.

While it may be tempting to merely patch together a rough box of corrugated metal, with a bit of effort and forethought, an outbuilding can actually enhance your property's charm and personality.

There are a number of ways to achieve this. You can purchase a prefabricated structure from a hardware store, hire a builder or an architect who may be amenable to taking on a smaller assignment, or design your own outbuilding based on plans from nineteenth-century source books, available at your library. They have simple designs and instructions that can be adapted for modern-day living and building codes.

You don't want an outbuilding to overwhelm the main cabin or distract from the surroundings. Take care to nestle the structure in a scenic setting and incorporate quality architectural or building elements, such as a gable roof or log siding. You may find that what began as a simple shed becomes a surprisingly appealing home away from home.

Facing page, top: This pampered pup—a hunting beagle with a nose for rabbits—is living large in his own log home. The dog house is constructed of leftover Norway pine logs from the owner's cabin and features a hinged roof that folds back, allowing it to be easily cleaned.

Facing page, bottom left: For a vacation getaway in coastal Massachusetts, an outdoor shower located on a walkway leading to the house is a practical innovation. Cleansing after a day at the beach feels like a welcome-home ritual.

Facing page, right: When the owner of this wooded property in Wellfleet, Massachusetts, asked her nine-year-old son what he wanted for his birthday, he told her he wanted his very own house. The boy's father eventually built three board-and-batten cabins—one for each of his sons. At 10 x 12 feet, these outbuildings are just big enough for a twin-sized bed, a chest of drawers, a desk and chair—and a wood-burning stove to keep them warm in winter.

Right: A tree fort in Hayden Lake, Idaho, is such an organic part of the surrounding forest that it features multiple trees growing right through the dual decks. This serene, screened shelter has proved ideal for naps and meditation.

The Do-It-Yourself Dream Home

A handy couple learns to build a cabin fit for their retirement

:: There are those homeowners who hyperventilate if handed a power tool of any description, and then there are folks like Chuck and Colleen Tralle, who took the concept of "DIY" to a whole new level when building their modest pine cabin on the banks of Minnesota's Barnum Lake.

The Tralles didn't fell their own trees or stack the logs themselves, but they did play an active role in all aspects of the project, from drawing their floor plan to slicking every last log inside and out with a protective sealant. "We're consummate do-it-yourselfers," Colleen explains. "There isn't much we can't do if someone has written a book about it."

This stone step was originally intended to be a bench, but it was the perfect height and shape to serve as a small landing to this side entry, which features a beveled glass window set in a distressed walnut door.

Peeled cedar stairway railings, complete with knots and evidence of worm tracks, contribute to the rustic interior atmosphere.

Chuck designed and built this cultured stone fireplace himself. The half-log coffee table was a housewarming gift from their neighbors.

SEEKING PEACE OF MIND

This enterprising couple found their land—a densely wooded acre shaded by birch and pine—in 1988. "It had a nice view across the lake to the Chippewa National Forest, and woods behind us that belong to the county, so that land will never be developed," Chuck explains.

The couple knew that they wanted a place where they could enjoy fishing, cross-country skiing, and cruising on their pontoon boat with their daughters and four grandchildren. "We wanted someplace secluded," Chuck says. Thanks to their isolation, their most frequent visitors are osprey, loons, and eagles, both golden and bald. "We also have raccoons and porcupine and bear," Colleen says, rattling off "bear" as if it were no more remarkable than "squirrel" or "house cat."

When they first bought the property, the Tralles lived 200 miles away. For six years, the couple and their three daughters, who are now grown and living on their own, drove up to spend weekends in a camper trailer nestled in a small clearing in the woods. They had no running water, no plumbing save for an outhouse, and no electricity for the first several years. But they did have peace of mind there on the lake shore.

"We were just dreaming about this being our retirement home and how many years we had to work before we could move up here and live a more relaxed lifestyle," Chuck explains.

A STREAMLINED PLAN

Unlike most folks, however, the Tralles like to relax with a paintbrush and a caulking gun. "The idea was that we would have a builder construct the shell for us, and we would take anywhere from 5 to 10 years to do the finish work," Chuck says.

To site their new home, the Tralles worked with a builder they met at a log home show. This builder developed some preliminary sketches, and then Chuck, who studied architectural drawing in college, adapted

The Tralles enjoy playing dominos at the kitchen table, or just gazing out the windows at the lake shore. Binoculars, handy for watching a resident pair of loons or the eagles that swoop majestically above the trees, hang at the ready beside the door.

Chuck and Colleen laid their kitchen flooring and assembled the spacious island themselves. In addition to storage for dishes and pots and pans, the island disguises a space-saving pull-out ironing board.

the plans in consultation with the general contractor they hired to construct the house.

Getting the house down to the size and budget that Chuck and Colleen wanted required reducing the size of the dining room, forgoing an additional bathroom on the second floor, and streamlining the shape of the house to avoid costly bump-outs. The result is a two-bedroom, one-bath home measuring just over 2,000 square feet, not including the basement.

"We didn't want more space than we needed for our daily lives, yet we wanted to be able to accommodate visiting friends and family," Chuck says.

BLENDING IN WITH NATURE

The house is built from round Norway red pine logs measuring 10 inches in diameter. The logs are milled and then shaped with an electric planer, giving them a rustic appearance at a fraction of the cost of actual hand-hewn logs.

The second floor is stick framed, encased with cedar lap siding outside and a combination of drywall and tongue-and-groove pine paneling on the inside. A teak-colored stain on the exterior gives the home a unified appearance that blends easily with the natural setting.

By September 1995, just three months after construction began, the basic structure was complete, but the Tralles' work was just beginning. With the help of their daughters and son-in-law, Colleen and Chuck stained both the exterior and the interior, scampering about scaffolding two stories above the ground.

The couple also did their own caulking, laid laminate flooring, hung drywall, built their deck railing, and constructed a 4-foot by 6-foot kitchen island that is large enough to accommodate food prep as well as Colleen's various crafts and sewing projects. But perhaps their most impressive undertaking is the sizable great room fireplace, which is flanked by asymmetrical display shelves and features an area for wood storage on one side.

And just how did they learn to do all this? "The way we learn everything," Colleens says with a laugh. As Chuck explains, "It's all through trial and error."

About this intimate window seat in the loft Colleen says, "The grandkids love it. They like to lay there and read books."

A Cabin off the Grid

Time stands still at this mountaintop farmhouse

:: There's no turbine powered electricity where Mark and LinaJean Armstrong decided to build their cabin, but the dramatic beauty of Hastings Mesa, just outside Telluride, Colorado, lets them indulge in their love of the outdoors—from hiking and skiing to cycling and fly-fishing in the pristine rivers and streams.

At more than 9,000 feet above sea level, Hastings Mesa is a remote and magnificent oasis hardly touched by the hand of man, and it's far away from the hustle and bustle surrounding the couple's primary residence in Atlanta. Sheep graze in the shadows of the towering San Juan Mountains, beneath Aspen trees and scrub oaks, and coyotes, wild turkeys, and black bear roam free. The air is thin and the snow is deep. At night, the inky sky is pierced by billions of white hot stars, distant balls of fire that flourish in the isolated darkness of the mesa, freed from the fierce, competitive glare of city lights.

South- and east-facing windows in the great room afford the Armstrongs a spectacular view of the San Juan Mountains, which boast one of the largest concentrations of 14,000-foot peaks in the world.

BASKING IN NATIVE AMERICAN HISTORY

Mark discovered the area several decades ago, drawn by his fascination with ancient cultures. "I was always an archeological nut," confesses Mark, a business executive whose job has taken him throughout Central and South America, where he's visited Mayan and Aztec ruins. In the United States, one of the most interesting civilizations that he learned about was the Anasazi, a population of Native Americans who lived in the Southwest for more than a thousand years. Their well-preserved, multilevel dwellings dot nearby canyons and Mesa Verde National Park. "It looks like the Anasazis packed their bags last weekend and left," he notes, though no one is sure of what drove them away. "They just vanished, and it's still a mystery."

From the Armstrong's perch atop Hastings Mesa, they have access to the ruins, the high desert, and the San Juan Mountains. "It is the most spectacular and the most severe range in the Rockies," Mark insists. LinaJean, who toured the Southwest in search of a second home site, agrees. "When I first saw the San Juan Mountains, I said, 'This is it. We don't have to look anymore.'"

Once the Armstrongs chose their site, they enlisted Telluride architect Ron Bercovitz to design a home that would suit their 40-acre sylvan spread while incorporating the character of an old farmhouse. "I had great childhood memories of my

Granite countertops and flagstone flooring in the kitchen are in keeping with Telluride's all-natural aesthetic.

"I designed that fireplace," says LinaJean, who chose stone resembling rocks found on the property. "I wanted it to look like it could have been gathered here." A Scandinavian carpenter, mindful of the cold stone hearth he grew up with, thoughtfully installed heat coils in the Armstrong's hearth for extra warmth.

here, which means using natural colors and natural products," notes LinaJean, who was adamant about using unprocessed or recycled materials wherever possible. "We used recycled Douglas fir wainscoting and timbers, and antique heart pine floors from Louisiana, which we laid upside down for that rough-hewn, farmhouse-type of floor. The older wood has more of a patina and richness to it," LinaJean says, "and I wanted that warm feeling."

The Armstrong's two grown sons stay in these cleverly designed guest quarters when they visit. Identical full-sized beds on each side of the room feature built-in drawers beneath and bookshelves overhead.

A guest bathroom features recycled, custom-made Douglas fir wainscoting and a 19th-century English fire bucket for a wastebasket.

grandparents' farmhouse," recalls LinaJean, who grew up in Lexington, Kentucky. "We took that concept and adapted it to the mountains."

ADDING TEXTURE FOR ANTIQUITY

The main body of the house, including the great room, dining area, and kitchen, is characterized by exposed interior timbers and simulated log siding on the exterior. To deliberately contrast the timber and log section, the architect designed the master bedroom and guest quarters with conventional framing and cedar siding. "The whole idea was to make the house look like it evolved over time," Bercovitz explains. The three-bedroom, two-bath structure is topped with a rusted steel roof, which, as Bercovitz points out, "blends with the browns of the landscape. It's more rustic, nothing bright."

"There's a more 'back to the earth' philosophy

ALTERNATE ENERGY SOURCES

In an area that receives an excess of 300 inches of snow every winter, Mark and LinaJean needed more than a cozy palette to keep them warm. Because the mesa is not part of an electrical grid, heat from the sun comes through large south-facing windows in the great room. These special windows are coated with a glaze that traps the sun's warmth. In addition, heat is generated by water that is warmed by two solar panels, and then piped beneath the floor. Household appliances are powered by batteries that store energy gathered from the sun, as well. A gas stove and a low-energy-consumption refrigerator reduce the demand on solar power, and a propane generator provides emergency backup.

Without an electricity bill to worry about, the Armstrongs can leave one more earthly concern behind when they visit their Telluride cabin. "It's so

beautiful and serene, it's like going to another world," LinaJean says. Even time seems to pass more slowly, and the couple is reluctant to leave this small slice of heaven behind. "I can go there for three or four days and feel like I've been gone for a month," she notes.

Mark agrees. "Living in this cabin is such a radical lifestyle change from Atlanta. It's a good cleansing agent, for the mind, body, and soul."

In this guest room, an antique American cannonball rope bed sports knobs on the headboard and the foot board. "In the olden days, they didn't have box springs," explains Lina-Jean. "They attached ropes to little knobs on each end of the bed, and the mattress sat on top of the ropes."

Bunking Lodge Style

After a long afternoon of hiking or fishing in the bracing water of a trout stream, you and your guests are probably looking forward to a good night's sleep in the comfort of your cabin. Create a bedroom or bunk room that is a memorable finale to an active day.

Although a four-poster is a tried-and-true cabin classic, you can literally branch out with a bed made from rough-hewn logs or even tree limbs.

For an added sense of intimacy, nestle your bed in its own little nook. If you like to wake with the dawn and catch the sunrise, install it in a window-lined cove.

To maximize your guest accommodations while minimizing square footage, build a bunk room. Installing a curtain that can be drawn across each berth will maintain privacy. You can accessorize the bunks with identical bedding or combine complementary colors and patterns to personalize each one.

Stretch bedroom space even further by adding drawers beneath bunks, where you can store extra blankets or where guests can stash their clothes. Or build a bed atop a platform that has storage underneath.

Log- and Adirondack-style beds aren't the only options for cabin owners who prefer a more organic look. This cherry headboard and footboard, which follow the natural contours of the tree, offer a slightly more refined alternative. The posts are constructed of chestnut barn beams.

This compact, efficient vacation home in coastal Massachusetts features just one bedroom for the whole family. In order to make the most of the sleeping space while maintaining a modicum of privacy, the architect designed a set of maple bunk beds for the children and a queen-sized bed with a curtain for the adults. A frosted door, leading to the home's living and dining space, fosters that implied sense of privacy while maintaining an open feeling, which is essential in a small space.

Bunking down in these log and twig beds is like camping out beneath the trees, but with all the comforts of home. Built-in benches provide a place to sit while changing clothes. The twig accents are also incorporated in the log lamp, the round window above the beds, and even the curtain rod brackets.

Appalachian Style

Childhood memories move one couple to re-create
an authentic Southern log cabin

:: As a boy, Dave Thomas remembers visiting his grandparents' 500-acre
farm in southwest Kentucky, playing beside the pond where their herd
of cattle came to drink, and working to preserve the Appalachian-style
log home where his father was raised. "We tried to keep the old log
home clean and keep it up," Dave recalls. "I really appreciated the values
those visits instilled in me for the outdoors, for working with your
hands, and for the ability to live independently."

His wife, Donna, grew up in rural Virginia with similar ideals. "We
very much like the outdoors and enjoy camping and hiking," Dave says.
With those pursuits in mind, the pair planted their roots near a stream
that feeds the Northwest River, building their own log home on a
densely forested five-acre parcel in southern Virginia.

The porch is equipped for casual entertaining, with rocking chairs, a log bench, and a barrel
that serves as a side table. Ax marks on the logs testify to the cabin's hand-hewn heritage.

A WARM WELCOME

With this piece of property, "We can pretty much do everything you might do in a state park," Dave explains. When they're not caring for their 30 bantam roosters, the couple can often be found hiking in the woods with their sons, Christian and Ryan, and their border collie, Poco. Their idea of relaxation is giving the rocking chairs on their front porch a workout, perhaps while deer-watching or savoring a steaming cup of coffee on Saturday mornings.

The casual, welcoming atmosphere they've created

is due largely to Dave's attempt to re-create an authentic Southern log cabin. "I wanted an Appalachian-style log home because that was what my Dad had, and also because, in this part of the country, that's what people would build," Dave explains. He took pictures of his father's childhood home to serve as a

Oak furnishings and a brass bed topped by a star-patterned quilt give this bedroom a timeless appearance in keeping with the "period" log home that Dave and Donna strived to create. "Most everything we collect is oak," Dave says, "because people around the turn of the century didn't have stores to go to." Mail-order furniture of the era was mostly oak.

guide and also visited several log homes in Highland County, Virginia, which is known for its wealth of antique log structures.

"Most of the log structures in Kentucky and Virginia are rectangular logs that are hand-cut, so round logs were out for us," says Dave, who was a stickler for detail. "We also wanted a tin roof and a front porch like they typically had, and a board-and-batten garage that looked like the additions they used to build when they had too many kids."

The Thomases selected a log home manufacturer that could provide hand-hewn logs based on traditional techniques.

"Houses today are out-of-the box—a lot of plastic and a lot of white," Dave says. But he and Donna "wanted something that was warm and real."

The Thomases chose a three-bedroom, two-bath style that has 24-foot-high cathedral ceilings in the

An upright piano stands opposite the front door, next to the home's hardwood staircase. Finding a prime location for a piano was a priority for this musical family. Donna is a piano teacher and a vocalist and Dave plays bass guitar.

great room and an upstairs loft. They selected logs that utilize a tongue-and-groove design that does not require chinking, though it can be added for homeowners who want that look. "We thought it would provide the best insulation and require less maintenance," explains Dave, who opted not to use chinking between the 6- by 12-inch rectangular hand-hewn logs. Dovetail corners and board-and-batten dormers provide additional Appalachian-style detailing.

"One thing we really liked about this house is that what you see is what it is," Dave says, noting that there are no "fake" rafters or beams inserted merely to enhance the room's rustic appeal. "If it looks like a beam that's supporting weight, then that's what it is," he attests.

The Thomases hired a general contractor to prepare the site and oversee all aspects of building the house, including designing a board-and-batten garage with an additional room above it.

When it came to preparing the building site, "We had the absolute bare minimum number of trees be removed to build the house," Dave says. "We've tried to leave everything as natural as we could."

The Thomas family did the site clean-up, and Dave installed river stone in the foyer himself. He also built the home's board-and-batten 2- by 6-foot plank pine doors and enlisted his sons to help him construct a striking half-log staircase leading to the second floor, removing an under-stair closet to showcase their handiwork.

Dave's willingness to barter a little blood and sweat enabled him to provide antique pine floors for the cabin as well. They rescued these from an old home that was being taken down nearby. "I talked to the guy that was doing the demolition, and I agreed to help him clean up around the site if he would give me what I wanted out of the house," Dave explains.

KEEPING IT SIMPLE

By March 2000, the Thomases were ready to move in, furnishing the home with unpretentious English and American antiques. Even the hardware on their doors hearkens back to pioneering days. "They're forged metal," Dave explains, because in the time period he wished to emulate "they didn't have doorknobs."

The vibrant grain of the custom built golden oak cabinets provides an eye-catching pattern, adding interest to the cabinets' clean-lined design and preventing the cabinetry from being overwhelmed by the tongue-and-groove ceiling and sturdy beams.

"Log homes didn't have a lot of trappings, so we tried to keep it simple," says Dave.

That same "keep it simple" philosophy extends to their leisure pursuits, as well. Christian and Ryan have built a fort in the woods, and Ryan has taught some local squirrels to eat right out of his hands. The family enjoys cooking out, too, and relaxing in a wooden swing on cool summer nights.

With this bucolic setting—and lifestyle—awaiting him at the end of a long day, "I like going home a lot more," Dave says with a laugh. "We hope never to move."

When building this log cabin, Dave sought to emulate the early Appalachian-style log homes that dot the Southern landscape. The interior décor echoes those simpler times, with a time-worn trunk serving as a coffee table and a rifle mounted atop a plain, unadorned mantel.

A Little Piece of the West

An unpretentious cabin getaway serves a family's sporting life

:: When Patrick and Sheila Rose built their log home in the heart of Montana's bucolic Bitterroot Valley, they knew what they *didn't* want. They didn't desire a lot of glitz and glamour, nor did they crave a cutesy interior design theme. All the couple required was a down-to-earth family getaway where they could spend quality time with their children and grandchildren and temporarily escape their hectic lives in Rancho Santa Fe, California.

When they visited a friend's house near the Stock Farm, a 2,600-acre golf and equestrian community flanked by national forest outside Hamilton, Montana, they knew they had found their perfect vacation home destination. "We've always lived in urban environments," says Patrick, but he and Sheila were drawn to the "down-home feeling" that Hamilton represented.

The great room is comfortably furnished with a sturdy leather couch and two Monterey-style chairs. A distressed console table, topped by a beaver pelt, introduces a rough-and-ready element of the old West.

The Rose's home nestles into the land's natural contours.
Chief Joseph stone, with its dusty shades of gray and brown,
was applied to the base of the home, grounding the structure in the rocky, mountainous landscape.

SHARING A LOVE OF THE OUTDOORS

Patrick was also lured by the Stock Farm's Tom Fazio–designed golf course and the first-class trout fishing river that runs through the valley. "Pat was learning to do fly-fishing, and I have a fly-fishing pole and a vest," quips Sheila. She and her daughters enjoy browsing the antique shops in Hamilton—and their young grandchildren love the horses, the Stock Farm's club-house swimming pool, and the community's little teepee where they camp out with their granddad.

They also frequently join Patrick on the river. "It's a big deal to have the grandchildren experience fishing, boating, and water rafting," Sheila says.

The basic style of home was dictated by the lot upon which the Roses chose to build. At the Stock

An old steamer trunk, which once belonged to Patrick's grandfather, provides extra storage for blankets and pillows in one of the guest bedrooms. Sheila found the chair at a shop in San Diego, then had it re-covered in a cow hide she purchased from a Montana taxidermist.

Farm—which is a joint venture between Charles Schwab, head of a national financial services firm, and Jim Schueler, president and founder of Rocky Mountain Log Homes—approximately one-third of the 125 homes planned for the development are required to be log. "The mountain lifestyle lends itself to log," explains Schueler, who has been producing log homes since 1974. "This community is really designed for the person that wants a little piece of the West."

Like all the houses in the Stock Farm, the Rose's home is a custom design. With the help of architect Jeremy Oury, they spent a great deal of time planning every last detail, from the placement of the light switches and electrical sockets to the flow of the floor plan.

"We wanted it simple, with the guest bedrooms on one end of the house and our bedroom on the other, with a big common area in between," Patrick says of the 3,100 square-foot, three-bedroom home.

THE LOOK OF PIONEER CABINS

In order to make it feel as though it had been built long ago, the Rose's paid homage to pioneer cabins from the late 1800s. A rich stain, which looks as though it has darkened over time, grants instant age to the 10-inch lodgepole pine logs and the rough board-and-batten siding that sheathes the gable ends of the house. Instead of opting for modern picture windows and a soaring loft, Patrick and Sheila favored smaller windows and a low-profile structure that hugs the landscape, anchored by native stone. "Everything we did was really driven by a desire to stick very closely to the period design," Patrick explains.

Inside, the Roses installed wide-plank, circular-sawn Douglas fir flooring that looks tough enough to withstand not only a trio of boisterous grandchildren, but a saloon full of rough-riders, as well. Gnarled character logs, a substantial stone fireplace, and a smattering of antiques and animal hides further conjure the spirit of the Wild West.

In the dining room, a one-of-a-kind light fixture provides an unexpected jolt of whimsy. Sheila sewed the cushions for the chairs. A German beer poster featuring dueling bears is a nod to the wildlife that roams the surrounding mountain ranges.

But Sheila, who handled her own interior design, wanted to create a home, not a Hollywood film set. "I didn't want it to be contrived or 'dressed-up cowboy,'" she explains. "It's fun to visit someplace like that, but you don't want to live in it."

AN ECLECTIC INTERIOR

To escape a clichéd interior, Sheila indulged her eclectic taste and made unexpected choices. A funky, futuristic row of pendant lights dangles above the dining table, and shimmering stainless steel encases the backsplash and the countertops in the kitchen.

The kitchen counters are sleek and chic, but the Roses also appreciate that they are practical, durable, and easy to clean up after one of Patrick's feasts. "I

love to cook," says Patrick, who often finds himself manning the stove for three generations of family.

"Our two daughters and their husbands and the grandchildren love the cabin," Sheila says. "The grandchildren play outside, climbing rocks and exploring and chasing birds. They talk about it all year long, and it's been fun watching them experience something totally different from California."

"Our grandson thinks that one of the ponies he rides every summer waits for his return the following year," Patrick says with a grandfather's proud chuckle. "If we can't live forever," he adds, "hopefully we can create a lot of warm memories that our grandchildren will always remember."

Stainless steel counters might seem an unusual choice for a rustic log cabin, but Sheila says it was a natural choice for them. "It gets a nice patina to it and ends up looking very old," she says. Black painted cabinets take on an aged appearance, thanks to lightly sanded edges and old-fashioned hardware.

Preparing a Cabinesque Kitchen

Depending upon how you use your cabin, your kitchen can be a tiny niche nestled into a corner or one of the most welcoming, widely used spaces in your home. A stripped-down bachelor's camp may require little more than a coffee maker, a toaster oven, and a microwave on a shelf above a dorm-sized refrigerator. But if your cabin serves as a base for entertaining and holiday feasts, or if you simply enjoy preparing meals, you'll need a kitchen that really cooks.

When you're whipping up a kitchen for a timeless retreat in the woods, there's a recipe for design success. First, begin by drafting a wish list of appliances. If you anticipate hosting many a Thanksgiving dinner, you may need not just one, but two ovens. Short-order cooks who like to serve big breakfasts for guests may enjoy using a built-in griddle that is perfect for pancakes and scrambled eggs. You can take your stove off the back burner by selecting a distinctive color or retro style to make it stand out in the space. Enclose the stove in a stone or brick niche to evoke the feel of the Colonial era, when cooking was done in an oversized fireplace.

Second, consider storage options. An antique hutch combined with simple open shelving and cabinetry made from reclaimed wood creates the impression that this space evolved organically over many years.

Finally, ensure that the kitchen reflects the personality of the cabin. Rough-hewn beams, wood or stone floors, and a mix of countertop materials such as soapstone and butcher block exude rustic charm.

Below: This kitchen makes the most of natural Western materials, in keeping with its setting in Steamboat Springs, Colorado. Hickory cabinets, white oak flooring, and an island faced in river rock befit the cabin's hand-peeled lodgepole pine logs. Built-in shelves accommodate detailed fish and duck decoys.

Left: Classic nickel plated appliances, coupled with a cultured stone backdrop, keep this kitchen grounded, despite subtle luxuries like the rosewood granite island countertop.

Facing page: This snug kitchen in Ashland, Ohio, could date from the early 20th century with its hand-hewn logs, apron front sink, and period stove. But the cabin, a weekend fishing getaway, was actually completed in 2004, and the erstwhile wood-burning stove hides a twenty-first century secret. It has been outfitted with electric elements.

Casting Call

Recycled materials create a timeless fly-fishing retreat

:: "My favorite quote about fly-fishing is that it's just enough of something to not be doing nothing," muses Mark Brooks. He grew up fishing with his father and uncle in eastern Louisiana and after moving to Atlanta, Mark often escaped the city on weekends to ply his skills in the streams of North Georgia and North Carolina.

But these rejuvenating waters were a long haul from his current home, where he lives with his wife, Shirlene. "I would get up at 4 o'clock in the morning and drive a couple of hours, fish all day, and then drive home," recalls Mark, who often logged 300 miles in a single day. "It was sort of a treacherous trip," he explains. "We started thinking it might make more sense to have a small place in the mountains."

Reclaimed wood from a tobacco barn frames a window seat, which is plumped with pillows stitched by Shirlene. A transom panel from an antique English door encases the area beneath the seat, hiding a sub-woofer and sewing fabric.

The foyer was specifically sized to accommodate a set of Peruvian floor tiles, which proves much sturdier than a rug. The paneling in the entryway is rough-cut pine, which Mark and Shirlene stained to give it an old patina. A framed photograph of horses, which hung in Mark's childhood home, was a gift from his mother.

A SITE BY THE STREAM

"We were looking for privacy, a getaway, and a feeling of remoteness," explains Shirlene, who grew up in the woods in central Maine and shares Mark's love of nature. "We wanted a place to relax and enjoy the outdoors."

A six-and-a-half acre plot in North Carolina's Tessentee Valley was last on the list the day they went searching for land with a Realtor. "It was further than we had planned to go," admits Shirlene, noting that this weekend retreat is about 120 miles from their main residence in Atlanta. "But when we got there, we both knew that this was it."

The property had the largest stream and the most acreage of all those they visited, and it was adjacent to the Nantahala National Forest. But it was the scene they encountered by the water's edge that really won Mark's heart that day. "The owner and his wife were sitting by the stream with a coffee tin of trout food, throwing it to the fish. There were twenty-five or thirty rainbow trout out there, and that was like a dream come true," Mark recalls with a laugh. "That really propelled us into action."

LIFE FOR LEFTOVER LUMBER

Both Mark and Shirlene agreed that they wanted the home they built there to reflect its surroundings. "We wanted it to look like it's been here a hundred years," explains Mark, who placed an ad seeking salvaged lumber and other reclaimed building materials in an agricultural newspaper.

His search eventually yielded a number of structures, including a log cabin, a tobacco barn, and a horse barn, all from various parts of Georgia. Shirlene, who guided the project through to completion, worked closely with their builder to find the best use for every scrap of reclaimed lumber.

They had the logs from the cabin sawed into paneling for the great room, chinking the spaces in between to evoke the feel of an old country cabin. Leftover portions were used for the stairs, a portion of the kitchen countertops, and other odds and ends, like a weathered shelf over the master bathtub. The tobacco barn and horse barn were also used as paneling and for cabinetry in the kitchen and bathrooms, and an old tin roof from yet another barn became wainscoting in the downstairs bath. Heart pine salvaged from a cotton mill was resurrected as flooring throughout the cabin.

The Brooks home is a blend of old materials—such as the log paneling which encases the interior of the great room—and new materials that have been given an aged appearance. For example, the rebar which adorns the curved balcony was left out in the rain to rust before it was installed.

"I was going for the lodge look—an old Adirondack style that was—most important—comfortable," explains Shirlene, who also scoured antique stores in search of interesting architectural elements. Among her finds were several old English paneled doors that feature resin deposits that glow red when struck by the setting sun, and a Peruvian tile mosaic that became the centerpiece of the entry foyer.

Any new materials they had to bring in were carefully treated to lend them the patina of age. In the foyer, for instance, the couple used rough-cut pine wood that they stained to blend with the antique barn wood. And when they decided to use rebar in place of balusters on an interior balcony overlooking the great room, Mark and Shirlene insisted that the builder leave the metal out to rust in the rain before he installed it. "We wanted it to look old," Mark explains.

A WEEKEND REFUGE

Since their cabin was completed, Mark and Shirlene find themselves making the trek together nearly every weekend, often accompanied by friends or family. Shirlene loves whipping up big meals, which she usually serves on their screened porch or on a spacious deck that encircles three sides of the house. An outdoor fireplace serves as a draw as well, especially in the evenings and at sunset. "When five o'clock comes around, it's time for wine and a fire outside," she says.

Shirlene also enjoys hiking in the woods, working in the garden, and watching the stream from an Adirondack chair at the water's edge. "It keeps our equilibrium," she says of the cabin. "It allows us to

Lumber from old buildings on the property was recycled to give the kitchen an old, lived-in look.

work hard during the week and know that the week-end is just around the corner."

As for Mark, this wooded refuge has proven to be a real fisherman's paradise. He now enjoys a mere two minute "commute" from the cabin, down a hillside filled with mountain laurel, to a stream teaming with trout. "It's made fishing a simple thing to do," he marvels. "I don't know anybody else who's got it that easy."

Thanks to a sizeable outdoor fireplace, the Brooks are able to extend their living space onto the deck year round. A stone drop hearth surrounds the fireplace, to protect against hot embers which may be expelled by the burning logs.

Stucco walls in the master bathroom were stained to resemble the chinking between the horizontal log paneling in the great room. Above the tub, weathered antique corbels support a shelf made from a scrap of salvaged log.

Pioneering Bathrooms

As a cabin owner, you don't have to rough it in the plumbing department, but don't feel obligated to install fancy marble vanities and gleaming chrome bath fixtures. A country cabin can be relaxed and a little whimsical, so take this opportunity to get creative with the once-humble "water closet."

For the biggest impact, incorporate unexpected elements in unusual ways. If you're wild for the West, fashion a mirror from a wagon wheel or transform a horseshoe into a towel hook. A fishing creel can serve as a repository for towels or toiletries, and a sink can be fashioned from a trough or a shallow bucket salvaged from a barn.

When it comes to cabinetry, think beyond the pre-fab units sold at the hardware store. Use an antique chest as a vanity, or nestle the sink in a sturdy slab of wood and fashion the cabinet from old barn siding. Complement the look with a vintage-style faucet.

Walls can be sheathed in weathered paneling, and a rusted tin roof may be pressed into service as a sink surround or a backsplash. By recycling old structures and enlisting items found in your attic or barn, you'll echo the thrifty ingenuity of pioneer homesteads, where nothing went to waste.

Finally, bear in mind that just because your bathroom may look deliberately primitive, that doesn't mean you can't enjoy a few hidden luxuries. When you've spent the day snowshoeing or skiing the slopes, you'll quickly warm to inexpensive innovations such as a heated towel bar and toilet seat, or even an indulgence like radiant heating beneath the bathroom floor.

Facing page, top right: By using rustic elements in an unexpected way, the owner-builders of this cabin in Creston, North Carolina, have created a bath that conveys a barn-like charm. The sink tucks neatly into a barrel, and a yoke has been converted into a mirror.

Facing page, top left: A hand-carved marble basin and dusky Venetian plaster walls add an elegant twist to this bathroom's Western décor. The sink sits atop an antique timber, arched to imitate the shape of the bowl, with a backsplash made from horse-chewed wood from a corral. Horseshoe towel hooks and lantern sconces continue the theme.

Facing page, bottom left: At this home in Telluride, Colorado, tumbled marble tile accents and real plaster walls provide a graceful counterpoint to the Douglas fir logs, which measure a minimum of 12 inches in diameter. From the Jacuzzi bath, the homeowners can enjoy views of the surrounding mountains.

Facing page, bottom right: Although this bathroom boasts all the modern amenities, witty touches—such as a cottonwood tree which doubles as a towel rack and toilet paper holder—give it a pioneering flair that fits its history as a century-old schoolhouse.

Left: This 1,200-square-foot log cabin, constructed on a bay peninsula in Santa Rosa Beach, Florida, was originally built as a guest home, but the owners were so pleased with the result that they opted to make it their full-time residence. Its amenities include a fully-equipped bath with an antique clawfoot tub and a separate stone shower faced in stone.

Living with Old-Fashioned Values

A childhood memory of Abe Lincoln's log cabin inspired one woman to build her own

:: For many cabin owners, the desire for a rustic refuge is a visceral pull, an indefinable longing that simply takes up residence in their subconsciouses one day and refuses to retreat. Some may struggle to define the exact moment that they knew they were destined for a woodsy sanctuary, but Wendy Wilson can trace her fascination with log cabins back to one tangible muse—a photograph of Abraham Lincoln that hung in her beloved grandfather's office.

As a child, Wendy was inspired by the tale of the young Abe Lincoln walking miles to return a few pennies to a customer he mistakenly overcharged. When she learned the much-admired sixteenth president was raised in a log cabin, Wendy began to equate old-fashioned values such as honesty and integrity with log homes themselves—and she resolved that one day she would build her own.

Bookshelves, framed by a decorative "flying eagle arch" overhead, flank a window seat, creating a cozy reading niche. The shelves are filled with everything from romance novels to tomes on Abraham Lincoln, whose log home captivated Wendy as a child.

This cabin's steel roof is coated with a thermoplastic fluoropolymer known for its gloss and color retention. According to Wendy, it's also a great asset when this northern-California region encounters severe winter weather. "The snow just flies right off of it," she says. A porch embraces the home on three sides, providing panoramic views of the mountains.

COMING HOME

Wendy found herself drawn to Yreka, a small, northern California town just east of Scott Valley, where her family once owned a ranch. She had invited her mother, Jane Cassady, to make the move with her, and she felt that for both of them, "it would be like coming home again."

One afternoon, as Wendy and her daughter were leaving Yreka, exhausted from a fruitless real-estate hunt, they spied a sign advertising two-and-a-half acres just within the city limits. "Mom and I went back up the next weekend, and she absolutely fell in love with it," Wendy recalls. Not only did the acreage offer exceptional views of Mount Shasta in the distance and a clearing where Wendy could build her log home, but it also boasted a 1950s-style ranch right next door for Jane.

Just as important, because of the area's harsh climate, where temperatures can drop below zero and pipes must be buried three feet down to avoid freezing, both homes would also enjoy the shelter of Forest Mountain and a variety of surrounding trees. "We have a lot of pine, oak, cedar, and some evergreens," says Wendy, who sited her home near the base of the mountain. "Because of our position, we don't get as much wind, but you get the full range of seasons."

FULL-SCRIBE METHOD

Because of her affinity for hand-hewn log cabins like honest Abe's, Wendy wanted a cabin with as traditional a look as possible. Her home, selected from a plan offered by a log-home manufacturer, is built with green logs, each hand-fitted to the log below. All the work was done with a chain saw.

A chain saw may seem like a crude tool best suited for felling trees, but in the right hands, it can be wielded like a sculptor's chisel. Even the most basic elements of Wendy's house are imbued with subtle, stylish nuances. For instance, at window and door openings, the thick, round logs are tapered to the width of the molding, creating a smoother, more finished look and "framing" the view. On the cabin's outside corners, the logs just beneath the eaves are longer, with each log closer to the ground cut a bit shorter, creating a flared "fish tail," as Wendy calls it.

Decorative tile work on the kitchen counters and bar-height swivel chairs upholstered in a colorful Southwestern pattern provide a bright contrast to the hickory cabinets. Wendy added the octagonal window over the stove in order to alleviate the linear pattern created by the log courses throughout the home.

The scene beyond the double-French doors takes center stage, without a television in the home to vie for attention. A scrolled log opening frames the view into the great room.

The master bedroom is outfitted with several treasured family heirlooms, such as a quilt made by Wendy's mother and a desk that once belonged to her grandmother. A square tile inset just inside a door leading to the deck allows Wendy to remove her shoes upon entering without tracking mud onto her creamy white carpeting.

She also incorporated several scalloped archways, known as "flying eagle arches," in order to soften the bold, straight lines of the logs and lend an element of architectural interest. The arches boast an added bonus by creating intimate reading niches that Wendy has flanked with bookshelves, where best-sellers share space with her grandfather's tomes about Lincoln. "I don't have a TV in my home; it's a conversation and book-reading home," she remarks. "I really like the fact that people come in to sit and talk."

BUILDING WITH RARE GREEN LOGS

One of the most unusual aspects of Wendy's 2,900-square-foot cabin is the logs themselves. The Douglas fir logs are massive, ranging from 16 to 24 inches in diameter. But what makes them truly special is the fact that they all come from the same stand of timber. "Since they were all growing in the same location, you have consistency of grain, color, and moisture content," Wendy explains. "That's very rare."

The logs were delivered in the spring of 1997, and within three days, the contractor and a log crew had completed the shell. By October, the home was weather-tight. Over the next several months, Wendy caulked and hand-brushed several coats of sealant on the logs herself, even though this sometimes required her to balance on 24-foot-high scaffolding. "My contractor said, 'Wendy, by the time you finish this, you're going to know every log and have a name for them, and some of them won't have very nice names,'" Wendy confesses with a laugh. "He was absolutely right."

By April 1998, the logs—which were cut green and allowed to dry naturally—had finished some of their shrinking, and the contractor was able to begin interior framing. In the summer of 1999, Wendy was ready to move in. "When the whole thing was finally done, that made me cry," she admits. "My sister, Janness, had a big sign across the garage door. 'Welcome home, Wendy!'"

"Home" is a slightly modified version of the three-bedroom, two-and-a-half-bath floor plan from the log-home company. Wendy enlarged the master suite and equipped it with a kitchenette, a separate outside entrance, and disability-friendly features such as a fold-down seat in an oversized shower, with the idea of creating a private haven for her mother if she eventually needs to move in. But for now, it's Wendy's own retreat.

AN ECLECTIC MIX OF WOOD

Throughout the home, she has created a warm, slightly eclectic feeling by combining various wood species and textures. For example, there are wire-brushed oak floors accented with decorative hobnails, hickory kitchen cabinets, cedar tongue-and-groove ceilings, and custom-ordered pine plank doors manufactured in Montana.

"It all seems to blend," says Wendy, who also found a comfortable mix of Southwestern, mission-style furnishings and treasured family heirlooms. In the dining room, for instance, her grandparents' ma-hogany table and chairs nestle up to a window seat plumped by colorful desert-sunset cushions, and in the bedroom, a couch with a Southwestern print keeps company with a quilt handcrafted by Jane and a desk and chair that once belonged to Wendy's grandmother. In the upstairs loft, her grandfather's framed portrait of Abraham Lincoln—the image that inspired it all—seems right at home.

Next to the soaking tub, fixed-glass blocks surround an operable window that is covered by a lacy white sheer, allowing in plenty of natural light without exposing the view *inside*. The large diameter logs are tapered down to the width of the window trim, demonstrating the handcrafter's workmanship and attention to detail.

Incorporating Character Logs

A character log is chosen to play a distinctive role in a cabin because of its unique, irregular qualities. Whether it's used outdoors as a porch support or indoors as a fireplace mantel or an accent beam that draws the eye upwards, the more gnarled, cracked, weathered, and worn a character log is, the better.

Two of the most popular types of character logs are "cat face" logs and burled logs. Cat face logs are typically created when an animal chews part of the bark off a tree, leaving behind a "scar" as the trunk heals. Burls are bulbous growths that occur on tree trunks or limbs. Their origin is somewhat mysterious, but they are thought to result from of a variety of causes, including freeze damage and infection. Burls are highly coveted because of

their interesting shapes and the rich and varied pattern of colors that are often evident in cross-section.

Character logs can be located through a variety of sources. You may find them on the Internet, through log home producers, or possibly through your builder. Some fortunate folks even discover worthy specimens on their own land.

Just keep your eyes peeled for imperfections and learn to flaunt those "flaws." Remember that the purpose of a character log is to lend your cabin a sense of organic legitimacy—to create a connection with nature by incorporating something wild and beautifully blemished.

Fantastically shaped logs, many from the owner's own property, are infinitely more interesting than traditional architectural columns, and better suited to this log home in Dandridge, Tennessee.

Left: Standing dead fir trees—killed by a fire on the owners' property—were reborn as distinctive support posts in this Montana log home. Their fire-blackened patina complements the gray recycled barn wood that faces the area below the breakfast bar, which features a three-inch slab of fir as a countertop. Pine and fir twigs, which were also gathered on the owners' land, add a personal touch to the balcony above.

Lower left: A juniper log, indigenous to this home's setting in the White Pine mountains of Arizona, is as much a work of art as it is a mantelpiece. The cultured stone fireplace proves a perfect match for the slate floors. Pine beams, approximately 12 inches in diameter, serve as structural supports for the porch's vaulted roof.

Lower right: Track lighting illuminates a cat face character log in the kitchen of this home in Sisters, Oregon. It is one of several dead-standing lodgepole pines, averaging 12 to 14 inches in diameter, which serve as structural joists.

Discovering Nooks and Niches

Remember how you loved snug, comfy spaces as a kid—like the window seat nestled beneath a dormer or an attic room with gnome-sized doors leading to storage under the eaves? Adults love these spaces, too.

By making the most of nooks and niches in your cabin, you not only answer the need for a private escape. You can also generate architectural interest in your house and transform awkward space into useful storage areas, as well.

:: **Create a sanctuary.** To cordon off a cozy retreat within a larger room, lower the ceiling height and add half walls flanking the entrance to this newly created alcove. Install built-in seating with bookshelves underneath to transform the space into a personal library/reading corner.

:: **Reclaim wasted space.** Use the triangle beneath your stairs for a closet or entertainment center. Salvage the space beneath the sloping, knee-high walls of a loft by installing a desk, a roll-out bed, or a stack of drawers recessed in the eaves.

:: **Look up.** For more nook and niche ideas, look overhead. In a bedroom with a cathedral ceiling, the area above a closet may accommodate storage for rarely used items or could be adapted into a tiny loft your kids will love. Just add a ladder to access this secret hideaway.

A guest bed in this Pennsylvania cabin feels secluded, despite being located in a loft, thanks to its niche beneath the sloping tongue-and-groove pine ceiling. The dormer window creates an inviting window seat with drawers for storage beneath it.

Left: No space is wasted at this renovated camp in Martha's Vineyard. Beneath the stairs, stepped cabinets store out-of-season clothing and extra blankets for cool evenings. All the milled wood throughout the home is made of vertical grain fir and cherry, and the floor is reclaimed antique heart pine. The ceilings were deliberately left low, in deference to the horizontal views outside.

Lower left: A wood-paneled inglenook provides a quiet hide-away that is somewhat sequestered from the adjacent great room, but close enough to the fireplace to hear the crackling of the flames. The bench seats provide a place to curl up and read, but they can also fold out to function as a bed.

Below: This guest cabin just outside Whitefish, Montana, offers easy access to hiking, fishing, and horseback-riding, and the mudroom entrance helps visitors keep hats, gloves, and other outdoor gear organized and at the ready. Distressed knotty alder cabinetry, inset with hand-hammered tin, make this space as stylishly distinctive as it is functional.

An Indestructible Log Cabin

A hand-hewn home is built to withstand the rough-and-rugged ranching life

:: As the manager of a registered Angus farm in Kentucky, Danny Rankin definitely feels at home on the range. His wife, Nancy, whose parents once lived on a farm, shares this love of the land and an informal, outdoor lifestyle. So when the couple decided to build their own home, they opted for a hand-hewn log cabin on five bucolic acres in Shelbyville, Kentucky.

Their hemlock cabin was inspired, in part, by a visit to a log home owned by some old friends. "We liked all of the wood, the open ceilings, and the hardwood floors," Nancy says. "We like Western-style artwork and clothes and big, massive, chunky furniture, and that sort of home just lends itself to that really well."

In the dining room, cowhide upholstered chairs and an antler chandelier mimic the rough and ready aesthetic of the Wild West.

DESIGNED FOR HARSH CONDITIONS

But the Rankins' cabin would be far from a cowboy museum or a furniture showcase. It would have to withstand the rigors of a rough-and-tumble ranching life.

One of their main requirements was a workroom between the garage and the kitchen. "With my husband being in the cattle business, we wanted to design it so that he could come in, take off his farm clothes, and have his own bath," says Nancy, who sketched the basic house plans herself. The room includes a washer and dryer, as well as Danny's clothes. "It's great, because he has his own space to get ready," notes Nancy, who doesn't have to worry about him tracking mud and muck through the house. And because the workroom is right off the kitchen, it can also serve as extra dining space when the couple hosts large gatherings.

Nancy and Danny wanted to build a kid-friendly home for their daughter, Bailey Joe, as well. This house

A set of hickory chairs and a rustic table beckon visitors to relax and enjoy the view from the front porch.

is "basically indestructible," Nancy insists. The center section of the house and the right wing are solid log, inside and out, and Nancy textured the drywall upstairs and in the left wing, where traditional framing was used. "With all that texture, if the wall gets a ding in it, it's not really noticeable," she explains.

INVESTING PHYSICAL LABOR

After an architect converted Nancy's sketches into architectural drawings, the Rankins took their plans to friends who were involved with the log home industry. Nancy and Danny loved the massive, hand-hewn logs available from one company, and they knew they could rely on the expertise of their friends for advice at every step of the process. Because the Rankins had decided to act as their own general contractors, they welcomed all the help they could get.

"[Our friends] did a lot of troubleshooting for us," says Nancy, who relied on her contacts to examine the architect's drawings and review bids from subcontractors. "[They] made sure people had included in the bids what needed to be included, and that we were charged a fair price."

"We have a lot more wrinkles and gray hair," after building the house, Nancy admits with a rueful laugh. But they "saved a ton of money" by managing the project themselves. She estimates that the total cost of her family's four-bedroom, three-bath house was about 40 percent less than the cost their architect had estimated.

They kept costs down, in part, by doing much of the physical labor themselves. "My husband tarred the basement, and he did all of the chinking by himself," Nancy notes with pride.

BUILT-IN SENTIMENT

The couple also shaved dollars, and added sentimental value, by refinishing six antique doors from an old log house that had belonged to Danny's family. The upstairs master bedroom also boasts a mantelpiece built by Nancy's great-great-grandfather. "My grandmother

Plaid cushions and a bold blue island add a splash of color to the cherry-wood kitchen.

Danny's father transformed this support post in the great room into a tiny cocktail table—and a great conversation piece.

The giant stone fireplace in the great room welcomes guests as they stroll in from the entryway. "People like to come here," says Nancy, who enjoys entertaining with her husband. "It's a real homey house."

salvaged it from the home she was born in right before they tore it down," Nancy says.

The Rankins' kitchen cabinets, baseboards, and window trim are all made of lumber harvested from a farm Nancy's parents used to lease. The farmer who owned the ranch sold her the wood, which he had stored for 15 years in a barn, for $250. Also, because their windows were cut to size on site, the Rankins were able to rescue the wood scraps for their staircase. "They were free steps," Nancy marvels.

But she and Danny didn't let their scrimping and saving affect the aesthetics of their home. To achieve the feeling of a rustic cabin, "it has to have hardwood floors, and it has to have a big old fireplace," Nancy says. The Rankins' home has both. The stone fireplace, with its simple wooden mantel, serves as the focal point of the vaulted great room, which flows in to the dining room and the kitchen, providing easy circulation for entertaining.

All of the rooms in the center and right wing of the home boast 10-inch-wide poplar planks, except

The loft is furnished with a table and chairs from Danny's grandfather and a daybed covered with a 90-patch velvet crazy quilt made by Nancy's grandmother.

the kitchen, which features ceramic tile. The tongue-in-groove pine flooring upstairs is actually the downstairs ceiling, as well. "There is nothing in between," Nancy says. "It's loud," she admits, "but I love the pine floors."

FEELING AT HOME

Nancy, who served as her own decorator, included several unique touches throughout the house, such as the metal banister and balcony railings, constructed with plumbing pipes, and the small, rustic table that Danny's father made to encircle one of the support beams in the great room. She also loves the look and feel of her dining room, with its cowhide-covered chairs and an assortment of small wooden shelves. These shelves were also crafted by her father-in-law and display an assortment of plants and memorabilia.

"I think the cabin makes people feel at home, and that's really important to us," Nancy says. "It turned out exactly as I envisioned it."

In the master bedroom, the queen-size bed faces a refinished rocking chair draped with an antique quilt from Danny's family.

"This guest room is kind of like 'the family heirloom room,'" says Nancy, who furnished it with her childhood hope chest and a quilt from her paternal grandmother. The red rocker and the 48-star American flag once belonged to Danny's grandfather.

163 ::

Fiddling around at Home

A beloved log cabin keeps this singer in tune with his patriotic spirit

:: The devil may have gone down to Georgia in one of Charlie Daniels's most famous chart-topping tunes, but when the singer/songwriter decided to put down roots and build a log home for his family, he found himself tempted by the rolling hills and peaceful pastures of Lebanon, Tennessee.

The year was 1976, and Charlie's reputation was already on the rise when the leader of the Charlie Daniels Band found himself drawn to a bucolic getaway on the outskirts of Nashville. His search ended the day he and his wife, Hazel, stood on a hilltop a half hour outside the country music capital of the world. They gazed out at a sizable pond, wooded slopes, and verdant fields that offered plenty of space for horseback riding.

"We've been able to carve ourselves a nice little niche," says Charlie, who has acquired 400 acres around Lebanon, Tennessee, over the last 30 years. "We can see for miles in all directions." Stands of poplar, maple, oak, and sycamore carpet the surrounding hills. From the front porch, Charlie and Hazel can gaze out toward their horse barn and the road that curves around the lake.

AN AMERICAN HOME

"We just fell in love with it," recalls Charlie, who was seduced by the quiet isolation and panoramic views of the surrounding countryside. "I go real big on gut feelings, and it just felt right," explains the Grammy award–winning musician.

Inspired by a pair of stately evergreens, he dubbed the ranch "Twin Pines" and soon broke ground on a log house. With its square-cut pine logs, thick white chinking, and wide porches supported by cypress posts harvested from his own land, Charlie's unassuming abode befits the patriotic guitar picker who remains, like the title of his 1970s song, a *Long Haired Country Boy* at heart. "There's something very homey about a log place," observes Charlie, who equates his simple, straightforward style to that of America's pioneers. And if there's one thing Charlie's fans know about the famous fiddler, it's that this man loves his country.

"I was a child of the Second World War, which was very real for us in coastal North Carolina," says Charlie, recalling how German U-boats patrolled the waters off his hometown of Wilmington, sinking American tankers bound for the European theater. Memories of the air raid drills, rationing, and blackouts that marked Charlie's childhood would later fuel his patriotic fervor, leading him to produce such hits as *In America* and *This Ain't No Rag, It's a Flag*. He has

"We had a guy draw up plans one time for a much fancier place than what we really wanted. It was beautiful, but we're pretty simple people, actually," says Charlie, who opted for the rustic look of chinked square logs. "Hazel is very, very big on flowers," Charlie says. With the help of their personal assistants Donna Copeland and Brud Spickard, they keep the yard blooming throughout the warmer months.

Hazel's antique fruit plates are displayed atop the hickory kitchen cabinets and quartz counters. A basket of her grandmother's rolling pins rests beneath an old butcher's block, which has graced the Daniels kitchen since the home was built in 1979.

even traveled to Iraq—twice—to entertain American troops fighting terrorism overseas.

No matter where he's been touring, though, Charlie always welcomes the sight of Twin Pines, tucked among the trees and drifts of blooming flowers. At 5,000 square feet, including four porches that look out over the fields where his horses and cows graze contentedly, the residence provides more than enough room for him and Hazel, especially now that their son, Charlie Junior, has a place of his own nearby.

DOWN-TO-EARTH INTERIORS

Despite its size, the home is hardly pretentious. With its combination of rustic country accents and American antiques, the décor tends more towards wagon-wheel lighting fixtures and vintage butter churns than Austrian crystal chandeliers and marble fountains.

Given their lack of outlandish luxuries, *MTV Cribs* (the television show that highlights celebrity homes) isn't likely to come calling—but that's just fine with this down-home duo, who have been married more than 40 years. "We built the place to suit us—not to be ostentatious for anybody else," Charlie explains.

"My taste runs to Western," he continues, as evidenced by his collection of Native American Kachina dolls, bronze cowboy statues, and Western-themed paintings that fill the spacious, peak-roofed den. This is clearly Charlie's haven, with his framed gold and platinum records filling whatever wall space isn't occupied by bookshelves crowded with Cold War spy novels and Louis L'Amour classics.

A CLASSIC CABIN KITCHEN

But the Daniels' preferred place to relax is the kitchen, whether they're bellied up to the dining table in a sunlit niche or kicked back in their recliners. Here, they are surrounded by the warmth of rough-hewn ceiling beams, knotted hickory cabinets, and honey-colored oak floors.

Of course, it's not just the atmosphere that lures Charlie to the kitchen; it's the savory scents of Hazel's cooking, as well. "One of my favorite dishes in the whole world is country-style steak," says Charlie, who also finds his mouth watering for his wife's biscuits, mashed potatoes, and pork chops. "Once we get off the road, we're pretty much into simple things," he says.

Charlie and Hazel: "We're working on 42 years (of marriage)," Charlie says of his wife Hazel, "and I tell you what, I'm ready to go for another 42."

In the winter, Charlie likes to build a roaring fire in the den's massive stone fireplace. Native American Kachina dolls parade across the mantel, and a trio of authentic Indian drums nestle beside the hearth.

During the holidays, Charlie rolls up his sleeves and pitches in, too. "I can make a cornbread dressing that'll make your tongue slap your eyeballs," he says, invoking the kind of colorful Southern-fried imagery that makes his lyrics so memorable.

More often, though, Charlie can be found picking out a tune on one of the guitars he keeps stashed around the house, fine-tuning his golf game on his putting green or driving range, or traversing the ranch on his four-wheeler. "If I come home and don't leave the place for a few days, it doesn't even bother me," he says.

"It's home, in the truest sense of the word," Charlie adds, a note of mellow satisfaction tempering the deep-timbered, rumbling voice. "I tell people when I leave Tennessee, I'm going to heaven."

"If you want to sit down and eat something or carve up a watermelon, this is a good place to do it," Charlie says of the stone patio.

The barn, which was built by Don Murray, one of the Charlie Daniels Band's former drummers, has been featured in several music videos. It is currently being renovated to house the Daniels' horses.

Resources

Contact information for many architects can be found through the American Institute of Architects, www.aia.org.

HONORING THE AMERICAN FRONTIER

Colorado

Architect: Edward Carson Beall and Associates, Torrance, CA, www.ecbarchitects.com

Project architect: Frank Balogh, Frank J. Balogh Architect AIA, Harbor City, CA

General contractor: Jim Messersmith, Jim L. Messersmith Co., Chatsworth, CA

Interior decorator: Susan Brown, Addison Interiors, Valley Village, CA

A CELESTIAL SKI RETREAT

Montana

General contractor: Doug Bing, Blue Ribbon Builders, Inc., Big Sky, MT, www.blueribbonbuilders.com

POLISHING A 1920S LAKESIDE GEM

Minnesota

Architect: Katherine Hillbrand, SALA Architects, Inc., Stillwater, MN, www.salaarc.com

General contractor: Dan Heikkila, Cromwell, MN, www.verndalecustomhomes.com

CREATING A CABIN GUEST HOUSE

Wyoming

Architect: Eliot Goss, Eliot Goss Architect, Jackson, WY, www.eliotgoss.net

Interior decorator: Chapman Design Inc., Houston, TX

A SIMPLE BOAT HOUSE

Maine

Architect: Robert Knight, Knight Associates, Blue Hill, ME, www.knightarchitect.com

A PLACE TO UNPLUG

Michigan

Architect: Mark Melchi and Ron Thomas, Archetype, Plymouth, MI

General contractor: Tim Powell, Handcrafted Homes, Inc., Saline, MI

A PASSION FOR PRESERVATION

Massachusetts

General contractor: Dale R. Nikula, Encore Construction Company Inc., Dennisport, MA, www.encoreconstructionco.com

AN ORIGINAL RIVERSIDE HOMESTEAD

Montana

Architect: Mark T. Johnson Architect Ltd. AIA, Kalispell, MT

General Contractor: Tim Stracener, Silver Wolf Homes, Kalispell, MT

BUILDING A CABIN FROM SCRATCH

Wisconsin

Design and construction: Ken Mattson (homeowner)

A LAKESIDE ESCAPE

Washington State

General Contractor: Bob and Rick Stockmann, SBC Construction, Bellevue, WA, www.stockmanbrothers.com

A CABIN WITH CHARACTER

Montana

General contractor: Gary Haskins, Haskins Construction, Inc., Red Lodge, MT

THE DO-IT-YOURSELF DREAM HOME

Minnesota

General contractor: Wes Hanson, Wes Hanson Builders, Inc., Merrifield, MN

A CABIN OFF THE GRID

Colorado

Architect: Ron Bercovitz, Bercovitz Design Architects, Telluride, CO, www.bercovitzdesign.com

Finishing contractor: Joshua S. Kent, Kent Building Company, Inc., Telluride, CO, www.kentbuildingcompany.com

APPALACHIAN STYLE

Virginia

General contractor: Glen Cameron, Henrico, NC, now retired.

A LITTLE PIECE OF THE WEST

Montana

Architect: Jeremy Oury, KIBO Group Architecture, Whitefish, MT, www.kibogroup.com

General contractor: Gene Mostad, Mostad Construction, Missoula, MT, www.mostadconstruction.com

CASTING CALL

North Carolina

No architect or builder information available

LIVING WITH OLD-FASHIONED VALUES

California

General contractor: Scott Kimball, Scott Kimball Construction, Yreka, CA

AN INDESTRUCTIBLE LOG CABIN

Kentucky

Interior decorator: R 2 Studio Inc., Lexington, KY

FIDDLING AROUND AT HOME

Tennessee

No architect or builder information available

Acknowledgments

Some of the material in this book appeared in different form in the following magazines: *Log Home Living, Timber Home Living, Timber Frame Homes, Log Home Design Ideas, Second Home,* and *American Cowboy.*

I would like to thank the editors of those magazines for introducing me to so many cabin owners who were willing to talk with me at length about their vision of the good life. There must be something about cabin living that draws folks who are invariably warm-hearted, down-to-earth, and gracious.

Thank you, too, to Tom Rosenbauer, Marketing Director, Orvis Rod & Tackle, for facilitating this book's publication under Orvis's esteemed name. Thanks also to Gene Brissie, Lyons Press associate publisher, whose idea it was to extend Lyons's Orvis publishing program.

Thanks to Maureen Graney, Editor-in-Chief of the Lyons Press, for giving me the opportunity to write this book, and to Marilyn Zelinsky-Syarto, who, along with Maureen, provided invaluable editorial advice. I would wager that you wouldn't be holding this book in your hands now if it weren't also for the contributions of photo editor Anna Adesanya and all the talented photographers whose images illustrate the simple, natural beauty of cabins across the nation. Thanks also to Nancy Freeborn, for her design vision, to Peter Holm, for executing it well, and to Chris Mongillo and Kevin Lynch for their production expertise. Finally, I am forever grateful to my family, for offering me their unconditional love and support. I'm looking forward to building more memories with you at our cabin.

PHOTOGRAPHY CREDITS

© Rob Karosis cover, Whitten Winkleman Architects, Portland, ME
© Roger Wade title page
© Brian Vanden Brink p.viii–ix, Stephen Blatt Architects, Portland, ME
© Amy Laughinghouse p.x (top)
© Brian Vanden Brink p. x Stephen Blatt Architects, Portland, ME (bottom)
© Larry Lindahl p.xi Last Dollar Ranch
© James Ray Spahn Photographer p.xii
© Roger Wade p. xiii Carole Sisson Design (top)
© Amy Laughinghouse p. xiii (bottom)
© The Orvis Company p.xiv
© Roger Wade p. xv Double Shoe Cattle Company, Centennial Ranch (top); High Country Builders (bottom)
© Christopher Marona pp. 2-9
© Roger Wade pp. 10-15 Blue Ribbon Builders
© Roger Wade p. 16 Yellowstone Traditions, Gandy Peace, Candace Tillotson-Miller Architect, Ruby River Ranch (left), JLF & Associates Architects and On Site Management (right)
© Brian Vanden Brink p. 17 Stephen Blatt Architects of Portland, Maine
© J.P. Hamel Photography pp. 18-25
© Roger Wade p. 26 Double Shoe Cattle Company, Dashwood House, Centennial Ranch
© Roger Wade p. 27 Double Shoe Cattle Company, guest cabin, Centennial Ranch (top)
© Brian Vanden Brink p. 27 Bullock Co. Log Home Builders. Tim Bullock 705-424-5222 (lower left)
© James Ray Spahn Photographer p. 27 (lower right)
© Roger Wade pp. 28-35 Teton Heritage Builders and Eliot Goss Architect
© Rob Karosis p. 36 Designer: Shirlene Brooks, Atlanta, GA
© Roger Wade p. 37 Noah Designs, Magaddino Architect, Denman Construction, and The Artisans (top left), Cushman Design Group (top right), Double Shoe Cattle Company, Dashwood House, Centennial Ranch (bottom)

© Rob Karosis pp. 38-45 Architect: Robert Knight, Blue Hill, ME
© James Ray Spahn Photographer p. 46
© Roger Wade p. 47 Honka Log Homes (top)
© Rob Karosis p. 47 Tiny Houses, Inc., Architect: Annette Lindbergh Putnam Valley, NY (lower left)
© Carolyn Bates p. 47 Dana Ennis, Ennis Construction, Inc., Ascutney, VT (lower right)
© Roger Wade pp. 48-53 Ron Thomas and Mark Melchi Architects
© Eric Roth p. 54 Clancy Designs, Jamestown, RI (left)
© FESchmidt.com p. 54 (right)
© Brian Vanden Brink p. 55, South Mountain Company.
© Jim Goodnough pp. 56-61
© Roger Wade pp. 62-69 Mark T. Johnson Architect
© Roger Wade p. 70 Heritage Log Homes
© Roger Wade p. 71 Double Shoe Cattle Company, Dashwood House, Centennial Ranch
© Roger Wade pp. 72-79
© James Ray Spahn Photographer p. 80
© Roger Wade p. 81 Real Log Homes and Vermont Home Specialties, Inc. (top)
© Eric Roth p. 81 Moskow Architects, Inc Boston, MA (lower left)
© Roger Wade p. 81 Appalachian Log Homes (lower right)
© Roger Wade p. 82 Double Shoe Cattle Company, guest cabin, Centennial Ranch (left), B.K. Cypress Log Homes, Anderson residence (right)
© Randall Perry Photography p. 83 The Fern Lodge, Chestertown, NY
© Roger Wade pp. 84-91
© Laurie Schendel Lane pp. 92-97 Neville Log Homes
© Roger Wade p. 98 Honest Abe Log Homes
© Roger Wade p. 99 Honka Log Home (top), The Old World Cabinet Company (bottom)
© Roger Wade p. 100
© Roger Wade p. 101 Expedition Log Homes (top)
© Eric Roth p. 101 Moskow Architects, Inc Boston, MA (lower left)

© Randal Perry Photography p. 101 (lower right)
© James Ray Spahn Photographer pp. 102-109
© Laurie E. Dickson Photography pp. 110-115
© Randall Perry Photography p. 116 The Fern Lodge, Chestertown, NY
© Eric Roth p. 117 Moskow Architects, Inc Boston, MA (top)
© Norman McGrath p. 117 (bottom)
© Roger Wade pp. 118-125
© Rocky Mountain Log Homes, Hamilton, MT pp. 126-133
© Roger Wade p. 134 Kuhns Bros. Log Homes (left), Montana Log Homes (right)
© James Ray Spahn Photographer p. 135
© Rob Karosis pp. 136-141 Designer: Shirlene Brooks, Atlanta, GA
© Roger Wade p. 142 Stone Mill Log Homes
© FESchmidt.com p. 143 (top right)
© Roger Wade p. 143 The Old World Cabinet Company (top left)
© James Ray Spahn Photographer p. 143 (lower left)
© Roger Wade p. 143 Yellowstone Traditions, Gandy Peace, Candace Tillotson-Miller Architect, Ruby River Ranch (lower right)
© Laurie E. Dickson Photography pp. 144-151
© Hearthstone, Inc. p. 152 Hearthstone Homes, Dandridge, TN
© Roger Wade p. 153 Carole Sisson Design (top), Expedition Log Homes (lower left)
© Swiss Mountain Log Homes p. 153 Swiss Mountain Log Homes, Sisters, OR (lower right)
© Roger Wade p. 154 Expedition Log Homes
© Roger Wade p. 155 Double Shoe Cattle Company, Dashwood House, Centennial Ranch (lower left), High Country Builders, The Old World Cabinet Co., and Hunter & Co., Homestead Lewis Cabin (lower right)
© Brian Vanden Brink p. 155 Hutker Architects Vineyard Haven, MA (top left)
© Roger Wade pp. 156-163 Appalachian Log Homes
© FESchmidt.com pp. 164-171

Index